Ghazali on the Principles
of Islamic Spirituality

Selected Books in the
SkyLight Illuminations Series

Ghazali on the Principles of Islamic Spirituality

Selections from *The Forty Foundations of Religion*—Annotated & Explained

Translation and Annotation by Aaron Spevack

Foreword by M. Fethullah Gülen

Walking Together, Finding the Way ®
SKYLIGHT PATHS®
PUBLISHING
Woodstock, Vermont

Ghazali on the Principles of Islamic Spirituality:
Selections from The Forty Foundations of Religion—*Annotated & Explained*

2012 Quality Paperback Edition, First Printing
Translation, annotation, and introductory material © 2012 by Aaron Spevack
Foreword © 2012 by M. Fethullah Gülen

Excerpts from the Qur'an in Aaron Spevack's annotations are drawn from *The Holy Qur'an: Original Arabic Text with English Translation & Selected Commentaries,* by 'Abdullah Yusuf Ali (Kuala Lumpur, Malaysia: Saba Islamic Media, 2000). Ali's translation is widely available online.

Library of Congress Cataloging-in-Publication Data
Ghazzali, 1058–1111.
[Kitab al-arba'in fi usul al-din. Selections. English]
Ghazali on the principles of Islamic spirituality : selections from Forty foundations of religion annotated & explained / translation and annotation by Aaron Spevack ; foreword by M. Fethullah Gülen.
p. cm. — (Skylight illuminations series)
Includes bibliographical references and index.
ISBN 978-1-59473-284-3 (quality pbk. : alk. paper) 1. Islam—Doctrines—Early works to 1800. I. Spevack, Aaron. II. Gülen, Fethullah. III. Title.
BP88.G47K513 2011
297.2—dc23

2011039874

10 9 8 7 6 5 4 3 2 1

Cover Design: Walter C. Bumford III, Stockton, Massachusetts
Cover Art: ©iStockphoto.com/Witold Ryka
Manufactured in the United States of America

SkyLight Paths Publishing is creating a place where people of different spiritual traditions come together for challenge and inspiration, a place where we can help each other understand the mystery that lies at the heart of our existence.

SkyLight Paths sees both believers and seekers as a community that increasingly transcends traditional boundaries of religion and denomination—people wanting to learn from each other, *walking together, finding the way.*®

SkyLight Paths, "Walking Together, Finding the Way" and colophon are trademarks of LongHill Partners, Inc., registered in the U.S. Patent and Trademark Office.

Walking Together, Finding the Way®
Published by SkyLight Paths® Publishing
A Division of LongHill Partners, Inc.
Sunset Farm Offices, Route 4, P.O. Box 237
Woodstock, VT 05091
Tel: (802) 457-4000   Fax: (802) 457-4004
www.skylightpaths.com

Contents ☐

BOOK I
The Science of Belief

BOOK II
Outward Actions

BOOK III
Purification of the Heart

BOOK IV
Meritorious Character Traits

Al-Ghazali and the Tradition of Islamic Renewal □

M. Fethullah Gülen

God Almighty, who introduces Himself in the Qur'an as the All-Merciful and the All-Compassionate, and deals with His servants on the basis of mercy and compassion, sent numerous prophets to humankind in order to convey His messages to them. God Almighty has equipped humankind with a mind, a heart, and certain other inner and outer faculties, and created the universe as a collection of clear signs pointing to Him so they can deduce the existence of God. However, since different factors can prevent these faculties from functioning properly, out of His mercy, He sent prophets in order to guide human beings to what is right and true in all areas of their life, and to happiness in both worlds (this life and the next).

In the terminology of Islam, a prophet is the one who communicates with God via Revelation, receiving messages from Him to convey them to people.[1] Among the prophets there are those called messengers who are given a divine scripture. Every messenger is a prophet, but not every prophet is a messenger. The scriptures or books that are given to messengers contain divine commandments or laws concerning individual life and social life with its various aspects.

The religion that the prophets communicated to people was always the same, with its basic rules of belief, worship, action, morality, and good conduct. It is based on submission to God Almighty and aims at peace and happiness in both worlds. The differences lay in its secondary aspects addressing changing times and conditions. Therefore, Islam commands the belief in all of the prophets and their scriptures as two of its essentials of belief; a Muslim is a follower of all of the prophets prior to and including the Prophet Muhammad, upon him be God's blessings and peace, who is the last of both the prophets and the messengers, coming with a universal mission and revealed book that is divinely preserved in both its meaning and its wording.

In the course of history, the followers of prophets strayed from the way of God, which was established and reestablished by prophets.[2] The flow of time came to the era of Prophet Muhammad, upon him be God's blessings and peace. God sent him for all people and revealed to him the Qur'an as the last of the divine books. However, this did not mean that the conditions all over the world would always be the same for the guidance of people and there would appear no deviations among Muslims. The only difference between the periods before and after Prophet Muhammad, upon him be God's blessings and peace, lay in the fact that the prophets or messengers prior to him were each sent for a particular people, and a new scripture was needed mainly because the previous one could be not preserved with its original meaning and wording. Prophet Muhammad, however, was sent for all peoples until the Day of Judgment and there would be no need for a new scripture because the Qur'an has been totally preserved, and the *sunnah* of the Prophet, the secondary source of Islam, was established.

Islam has come face to face with new conditions, and deviations and conflicts have appeared among Muslims. In addition to this, when Islam spread quickly in the lands where many other religions and philosophies either appeared or spread, it found itself in a position of both preserving its very existence and answering the doubts and questions put to it by other religions and philosophies. All these and several other factors have caused the birth of religious sciences such as jurisprudence, the science of studying the prophetic traditions, interpretation of the Qur'an, and Islamic theology. Also born was what has been called Sufism, which focuses on improvement of the soul, spiritual perfection, and studying the inner dimension of Islam. With the contribution of great advancements in natural and experimental sciences such as physics, chemistry, medicine, and astronomy, these religious sciences and Sufism lay the groundwork and became the most propitious source for the magnificent Islamic civilization, which lasted many centuries.

Thus, in the absence of divinely guided and protected prophets after the Prophet Muhammad, upon him be God's blessings and peace, both the great Muslim scholars and the spiritual guides (commonly called the Sufi masters) have performed in the history of Islam almost the same function as the prophets in previous periods, despite their lacking the prophetic qualities such as sinlessness and freedom from mental or physical impediment. They have guided people in understanding Islam correctly, educating them both mentally and spiritually and in practicing Islam in their daily lives.

However, there have been times when deviations in either belief and thought or practice—or both—have spread widely and deeply. In those times, out of God's mercy, there have appeared greater scholars, spiritual masters, saintly scholars—who have combined both scholarship and spiritual mastery—or even greater statesmen. They have restored the true Islamic standing or position in matters of politics, revived true Islamic government, cleansed Islamic thought and belief of un-Islamic elements that had filtered in from other religions or philosophies, or given a new, accurate impetus to Islamic life. They have been called revivers or renewers in Islamic terminology.[3] According to many researchers and Muslim historians, Imam Abu Hamid Muhammad ibn Muhammad al-Ghazali (1058–1111), author of *The Forty Foundations*, is considered among the most famous and most widely accepted ones.[4]

Although Imam al-Ghazali lived during the years when the Seljuk rule brought stability to the Muslim world, due to the seditious and corrupt actions of some sects that were known as esotericist, such as the Karamatis, and certain heretical groups, political turmoil and inner clashes did not cease. These turmoils and clashes caused moral degenerations, neglect of Islam's everyday practices, and doubt concerning certain Islamic beliefs.

In addition, Hellenistic and/or Greek philosophy influenced some universally famous Muslim minds, such as Ya'qub ibn Ishaq al-Kindi (Latin: Alkindus) (801–873), who is known to be the first to introduce Greek and/or Hellenistic philosophy into Islamic thought; Abu Nasr al-Farabi (Latin: Alpharabius) (872–951) in the East; and Abu Bakr Muhammad ibn Yahya ibn Bajja (Latin: Avempace) (1085–1138) and Abu'l-Walid Muhammad ibn Ahmad ibn al-Rushd (Latin: Averroes) (1126–1198) in the West. These famous polymaths, who are known as the Muslim Peripatetics, tried to reconcile Islamic belief with Aristotelian rationalism and explain the Divine Being, creation, and the relationship between the Divine and the created world using certain terminology and elements borrowed mostly from Greek thought that have usually been referred to as "rationalistic."

In addition to the Muslim Peripatetic philosophy, two other currents of thought were influential in the years when al-Ghazali lived. One of them was Islamic theology and the other was what has been called Avicennism, which was represented by another great Muslim polymath, Abu Ali Husayn ibn Sina (Latin: Avicenna) (980–1037), and augured the Muslim illumination of Shahab al-Din al-Suhrawardi (1155–1191). Both Islamic theology and illumination have generally been regarded as the combination or reconciliation of purely Islamic thought with a modified Neoplatonism and Aristotelian rationalism.

Prior to al-Ghazali's age, many important works had already appeared that explained Sufism, not as a different way of thinking or a unique lifestyle of certain individual Muslims, but rather as a branch of the Islamic sciences.[5] Al-Ghazali studied all the schools of thought mentioned and discussed them in his *Deliverance from Error*. He described how he was delivered from their errors and found the ultimate value in Islamic Sufism, not as a special way of belief and life, but as the way of Islam itself, which combines shariah and spirituality into one inclusive body.

Al-Ghazali was brought up in such a climate and, after a good education, found himself as a world-renowned professor in the Baghdad branch of the Nizamiyyah school.[6] Being a reviver or renewer so wise, intelligent, and well versed in jurisprudence and its principles, Islamic theology, and philosophical thought, al-Ghazali played two major roles in Islam. First, he wrote *The Incoherence of the Philosophers* and successfully changed the course of Muslim thought and extirpated Greek thought, removing its effects from Muslim minds. His success in refuting the early Islamic Aristotelian rationalism and Neoplatonism by showing their contradictions was to the extent that they have not been able to recover since, and authentic Islamic belief gained great strength in minds and hearts. Al-Ghazali's popularity, gained by his lectures in the Baghdad Nizamiyyah school, certainly contributed to his dramatic defeat of the Muslim adaptation of Greek philosophy.[7]

The second major role that al-Ghazali played as a Muslim renewer or reviver is in achieving, as Dr. Spevack describes, "a balanced perspective on incorporating the teachings of all three sciences into one's religious life, without contradicting the orthodox tenets of law or theology in the process." The two aspects of the same truth—the commandments of shariah and Sufism—have sometimes been presented as mutually exclusive. This is quite unfortunate, because Sufism is nothing more than the spirit of the shariah, which is made up of austerity, self-control, and criticism, and the continuous struggle to resist the temptations of Satan and the carnal, evil-commanding soul in order to fulfill religious obligations. Both Sufis and scholars sought to reach God by observing the divine obligations and prohibitions. Nevertheless, some extremist attitudes—occasionally observed on both sides—caused disagreements.[8]

In fact, Sufism and jurisprudence are like the two schools of a university that seeks to teach its students the two dimensions of religion so that they can practice it in their daily lives. One school cannot survive without the other, for while one teaches how to pray, be ritually pure, fast, give charity, and regulate all aspects of daily life, the other concentrates on what these and other actions really mean, how to make worship an inseparable part of one's existence, and how to elevate each individual to the rank of a universal, perfect being—a true human being. That is why neither discipline can be neglected. In the words of Dr. Spevack, *The Forty Foundations of Religion* "seeks to expound on the essence of the Qur'anic teachings ... and represents al-Ghazali's effort to express the teachings of the three dimensions of Islam (faith, practice, and spiritual perfection) in a way that harmonizes all three dimensions of theology, law, and Sufism."

It is worth high appreciation and gratitude that at a time when incorrect interpretations of religions, even among their followers, are still dominant in the world despite great advancements in the means of transportation and communication, al-Ghazali's *The Forty Foundations of Religion* has been translated by a respected specialist in the fields that the great Imam al-Ghazali mastered, namely Islamic jurisprudence, Islamic theology, and Sufism. It is my hope that Dr. Spevack, being not only a specialist in these fields but also a musician and an activist in interfaith dialogue, will continue to render other great services in correct understanding of religions, especially the religion of Islam in the West, and bring peoples of different faiths and cultures closer to each other. Together with my sincere thanks and appreciation, I express my due regards and good wishes for him.

Introduction ☐

Abu Hamid al-Ghazali, the great Persian polymath of the twelfth century, is considered one of the greatest scholars of Islam. He was a master of several Islamic sciences, including law, theology, philosophy, and Sufism (Islamic spirituality). Despite his scholarship in multiple sacred sciences, his most far-reaching contribution in the Muslim world was his synthesis of the sciences of Islamic law, theology, and Sufism. His views on the interconnectedness of these three sciences and his justification for the orthodox status of Sufism is found in his multivolume and hugely popular work *The Revival of the Religious Sciences*. His impact was not limited to Islamic scholarship, however. His writings on philosophy and theology impacted Jewish and Christian scholarship, including the works of Maimonides and Saint Thomas Aquinas.

A Life of Law, Science, and Spirituality

Al-Ghazali was born sometime between 1056 and 1059 CE during a period of intense theological rivalry between the Ash'ari school of thought, which championed the beliefs of Sunni Islam using rational theology, and the Mu'tazili school of thought, whose rationalism led them to adopt a number of opinions at odds with the Sunnis. Among the opinions held by the Mu'tazilis that differed from the Sunnis was the belief that the descriptions of heaven's pleasures and hell's pains were not literal, but metaphorical. The Sunnis, on the other hand, considered them to be literal, though with a reality that can only be experienced. At age thirteen, al-Ghazali began intensive study of the Islamic sciences in his native Tus in modern-day Iran and later entered the prestigious Nizamiyyah Islamic college (*madrasah*) in Nishapur, the capital city of Khorasan. Among his most famous teachers was al-Juwayni (d. 1085 CE), a well-known and highly influential scholar of law and theology.

By 1063 CE, al-Juwayni and the Ash'arites had won the day, and Ash'ari theology dominated the centers of Islamic learning in Nishapur and elsewhere. Al-Ghazali was deeply rooted in, though at times critical of, the Ash'ari school of theology. In matters of law, he was a highly qualified master of the teachings of the Shafi'i school of law, one of the four predominant Sunni schools of Islamic law (*fiqh*). Indeed, al-Ghazali's efforts in the Shafi'i school had a major impact on the later recension and application of the school.

Beginning in the 1070s, the Seljuk Turks had come to power in much of the Islamic heartlands, including Anatolia, Khorasan, and the Levant, corresponding to parts of modern-day Turkey, Iran, Afghanistan, Jordan, Syria, Israel, Palestine, and beyond. Under Seljuk rule, the powerful vizier Nizam al-Mulk (d. 1092 CE) increased in power and influence. Among his goals was to strengthen Sunni Islam, in opposition to the various sects of Shia Islam that had come to power in the tenth century in places like Egypt and elsewhere.[1] Al-Ghazali became associated with the Seljuk sultan's court sometime in the 1070s and eventually came under the support of Nizam al-Mulk. Sometime in the 1080s, al-Ghazali was situated in the city of Isfahan, and upon being appointed to the top position at Baghdad's Nizamiyyah college, he found himself living in what had been for centuries one of the primary centers of Islamic learning. It was in Baghdad that al-Ghazali eventually wrote his famous refutation of Greek and Greek-influenced philosophy, titled *The Incoherence of the Philosophers*, which refutes specific unsubstantiated metaphysical doctrines held by ancient Greek philosophers and the Muslim (and non-Muslim) philosophers of the Islamic empires.

In that same year, al-Ghazali had a crisis of faith, so intense as to impede his ability to teach at the Nizamiyyah college. It was a time of political turmoil; Nizam al-Mulk had been assassinated a few years earlier, presumably by a follower of a radical branch of the Ismaili Shia, a sect with whom al-Ghazali incidentally takes issue in a number of his works. Some Muslim scholars attribute al-Ghazali's departure from Baghdad to the political exigencies of the time; however, in his own writings, he indicates it was due to his crisis of faith. Disillusioned with his scholarly life thus far, which had been supported by associations with powerful courts and institutions, he left in order to fully dedicate himself to the mystical path of Sufism.

Traveling to Damascus, then to Jerusalem, then to Mecca on the Hajj (the religiously required pilgrimage), then back to Damascus, al-Ghazali devoted himself to the study and application of Sufism in hopes of achieving the high spiritual states to which it calls. While in Damascus, he secluded himself in the minaret of the Great Mosque of Damascus and later did the same thing in the Dome of the Rock in Jerusalem, spending his time devoted to the remembrance of Allah (*dhikr*) and other Sufi exercises. It was during this time that he wrote *The Revival of the Religious Sciences*.

After a few years, in 1096, al-Ghazali left Damascus—largely because of the insistence of his children—and returned to Baghdad, reading publicly his *The Revival of the Religious Sciences*. In the absence of the technology to mass-publish works upon completion, public readings were a common means of transmitting scholarship, in addition to the production of manuscripts. Soon after, he made his way back to his hometown of Tus, where he would stay for several years. Having vowed to avoid teaching in state-sponsored institutions, thereby avoiding the risks of teaching sacred knowledge for worldly gain, al-Ghazali had been teaching in privately funded schools in Damascus. After settling in Tus, he founded his own school and Sufi convent (*khanqah*). By 1106, however, he was back to teaching in the Nizamiyyah, at the demand of the sultan, this time in Nishapur, where he had been a student of al-Juwayni so many years earlier. Despite having forsworn teaching in state-sponsored institutions, al-Ghazali justified his return, arguing that the need to combat various theological controversies outweighed his desire to teach only in private institutions. Al-Ghazali died in the year 1111 CE and was buried in Tus, where he had continued to teach up until his death.

Al-Ghazali's Writings

Al-Ghazali was a prolific writer, with an estimated seventy works of varying length. He began his academic efforts with the study of law and therefore wrote much on this topic, including *The Concise Abridgment Regarding the Legal Deductions of al-Shafi'i*.[2] He also wrote on theology, including his work *Warding Off the Masses from the Sciences of Theology*, which sought to keep the average worshipper at a safe distance from the controversial topics of theology that had resulted in the formation of dif-fering sects or scholarly divisions within Sunni Islam. He wrote works on logic, such as the *Criterion of Knowledge in the Art of Logic*, and on phi-losophy, culminating in his aforementioned book, *The Incoherence of the Philosophers*.

Later in his career, he composed several works on the Sufi path, and although there is substantial overlap in the content of these works, they have different aims or audiences in mind. *The Revival of the Religious Sciences* is a comprehensive exposition of all that al-Ghazali has to say on the matter of Sufism, which is presented as inextricably linked to Islamic law and theology. It is geared toward the scholar who is committed to studying its many chapters and subdivisions. *The Jewels of the Qur'an*, which includes *The Forty Foundations of Religion* as its introduction, expounds on the essence of Qur'anic teachings and, with regard to *The Forty Foundations of Religion* in particular, summarizes the core teach-ings of *The Revival of the Religious Sciences* in forty foundational matters. It appears to be geared toward a readership comprising scholars, students of sacred knowledge, and educated laypeople, whose education was nonetheless often quite extensive. *The Alchemy of Happiness* is also a summary of *The Revival of the Religious Sciences* and *The Forty Foundations of Religion*, but it is written for a Persian-speaking, rather than Arabic-speaking, audience. Upon returning to teaching in Nishapur, after his years spent traveling the Sufi path in Damascus and Jerusalem, al-Ghazali was also compelled to return to the subject of law, specifically the foundations of deriving laws, and wrote a detailed book on Islamic legal theory. That one of his later writings was on legal matters is indicative of al-Ghazali's spirituality; Sufis do not abandon the law upon achieving spiritual perfection.

Al-Ghazali's *The Revival of the Religious Sciences*

It has been said that if all the secondary texts of Islam were to disappear, *The Revival of the Religious Sciences* would suffice. The book, which fleshes out in great detail al-Ghazali's views on Islamic law, theology, and especially Sufism, is divided into four main sections and is usually published in four or more volumes, each consisting of several hundred pages. The first quarter deals with matters of worship, the second with issues pertaining to etiquette and daily life, the third with the ruinous traits, and the fourth with the ways of salvation.

Written in the eleventh century, *The Revival of the Religious Sciences* initially met with some resistance in parts of North Africa, because many of the scholars of the region had an unwavering bias for the Maliki school of law and the Ash'ari school of theology, with whose founders al-Ghazali at times respectfully disagreed. It was also criticized by some scholars for errors in narration of hadith, the recorded sayings of Prophet Muhammad, and for delving into matters of spiritual experiences whose authenticity and legitimacy was debated. However, despite these problems and the debate over the meanings of the technical terms referring to Sufi experiences, even critics could not help but appreciate the overwhelming content with which they agreed. *The Revival of the Religious Sciences* has been translated into many languages and continues to be studied and taught today around the world.

The Forty Foundations of Religion

The Forty Foundations of Religion is al-Ghazali's own abridgment of *The Revival of the Religious Sciences*. Like *Revival*, it was written in the eleventh century, after al-Ghazali experienced a crisis of faith, and is therefore deeply imbued with the Sufi thought this crisis led him to study and apply. Though less known than *Revival*, it covers similar content but is more accessible because of its smaller size. Throughout *The Forty Foundations*, al-Ghazali often refers the reader to *Revival* for further study.

The Forty Foundations of Religion, as mentioned previously, was written as an introduction to al-Ghazali's work *The Jewels of the Qur'an* and was considered by al-Ghazali to contain the essence of the Qur'anic teachings. Presumably, the reader must first understand the content of *The Forty Foundations of Religion* in order to have a solid understanding of the Qur'anic wisdom presented in the balance of the work. Since this introduction could stand on its own, al-Ghazali gave permission for it to be read and published as a separate work.

Along with *The Revival of the Religious Sciences*, *The Forty Foundations* represents al-Ghazali's effort to express the teachings of the three dimensions of Islam—law, theology, and spirituality—in a way that harmonizes all three dimensions. Before al-Ghazali's time, scholars of law often found fault with some Sufi practices, while scholars of theology often found fault with Sufi terminology and metaphysics. In *Revival* and *The Forty Foundations*, al-Ghazali offers a balanced perspective on incorporating the teachings of all three sciences into spiritual life, without contradicting the orthodox tenets of law or theology in the process. As a result of his effort, al-Ghazali is often considered the person responsible for justifying Sufism within an orthodox framework; however, it may be more apt to describe him as the one who most succinctly summarized and expounded upon the orthodox conceptions of law, theology, and Sufism, which had already been viewed by many as necessarily linked prior to al-Ghazali's time.

The Three Dimensions of Islam

The three dimensions of Islam—*Islam, Iman, Ihsan*—might be translated as "law, theology, and spirituality" or as "submission, faith, and spiritual perfection." They form the core of Islam, and to have one without the others is at best imperfect and at worst invalid.

The Dimension of *Islam* and the Five Pillars of Ritual and Practice

The first dimension, *Islam*, meaning "submission," lays out the five foundational matters or pillars of ritual and practice. In *The Forty Foundations*, al-Ghazali addresses some of the spiritual secrets associated with the five pillars.

The first pillar, the testification of faith (*shahadah*), is to verbally declare that there is no deity worthy of worship other than Allah and that Muhammad is His messenger. It is a spoken declaration and must be stated before witnesses in order to enter into the societal folds of Islam. Upon "taking your *shahadah*," you enter into the rights and responsibilities of Muslims. For example, a Muslim is required to pay the poor tax (*zakah*) if his or her saved wealth remains at or above a specific threshold for a full lunar year. Thus, when you take the *shahadah*, you are then legally obligated to pay the *zakah* if applicable. The full testification of faith is "I declare there is no God but Allah, and I declare that Muhammad is the messenger of Allah" (*ashhadu ann la ilaha illAllah, wa ashhadu ann muhammadan rasulullah*).

The second pillar comprises the five daily ritual prayers (*salah*). These are prayed at specific times of day and require that you be in a state of ritual purity, obtained through performing ablutions. The ritual prayer consists of recitation of the Qur'an and a series of movements, including standing, bowing, and prostrating. It is a means of purifying your soul, remembering Allah and your ultimate purpose, and unifying people in the worship of Allah.

The third pillar is fasting in the Islamic lunar month of Ramadan, which entails abstaining from food, drink, and sexual intercourse from the first light of dawn until sunset. It is a means of humbling the ego, drawing nearer to Allah, instilling thankfulness in the worshipper, and building a sense of camaraderie between those who have and those who have not.

The fourth pillar, *zakah*, is giving 2.5 percent of your stored wealth to the poor, needy, and other specific recipients. It is a means of purifying your wealth of intentional or inadvertent ill-gotten gains. It is also a means of supporting the less fortunate in society. Islam is community based, rather than an individualistic faith.

The Hajj, a once-in-a-lifetime pilgrimage—for those financially and physically able—to Mecca in modern-day Saudi Arabia, is the fifth pillar. It is not merely a journey to a destination, but rather an involved series of rites commemorating the experience of the Prophet Abraham and his family in Mecca.

Also associated with the dimension of *Islam* are physical actions that you perform in private or public. From the viewpoint of Islamic law, there are five types of action: obligatory, recommended, neutral, disliked, and prohibited. Obligatory matters are rewarded in the afterlife if performed, and punished if neglected. Recommended matters are rewarded if performed, but not punished if neglected. Neutral matters have no reward or punishment associated with them. Disliked matters are not punished if performed, but rewarded if avoided. Prohibited actions are punished if performed, and rewarded if avoided. Therefore, there are commands and prohibitions related to food, dress, marriage, divorce, family matters, inheritance, commerce, politics, and so on. All of these pertain to actions of the body, and therefore the dimension of *Islam* deals with the physical body as it relates to worship and society.

The Dimension of *Iman* and the Six Core Articles of Faith

While the dimension of *Islam* pertains to the body, the second dimension of Islam, *Iman*, pertains to the mind. It outlines the six core beliefs in which a Muslim must have firm faith. Al-Ghazali devotes most of his attention to the first article of faith—belief in Allah—in book 1 of *The Forty Foundations of Religion* and assumes knowledge of the remaining throughout. The six articles of faith are explained as follows:

1. The belief in Allah, the one and only God: According to Muslim scholars, you must know the following about Allah: He exists, has no beginning, has no ending, is absolutely independent, is totally dissimilar from His creation, is totally singular in every regard, and has the attributes of Power, Will, Knowledge, Life, Hearing, Sight,

and Speech. Their opposites are inconceivable for Him (i.e., ignorance, powerlessness, nonexistence). Possible with regard to Allah is His creating the universe in nonexistence, meaning that He was in no way compelled to create anything. How these attributions are in reality is known to Allah alone.

2. The belief in the prophets and messengers: Muslims believe that throughout human history Allah has sent certain honest, obedient, highly intelligent individuals, whom He chooses, and inspires them with commands and prohibitions, which they necessarily transmit. Prophets (*anbiya'*) are those who have received revelation from Allah—which may entail reaffirming a previous prophet or supporting a concurrent prophet or messenger (*rasul*). Messengers are prophets who have received a revealed book. Throughout *The Forty Foundations*, "prophet" and "messenger" are used interchangeably, as Muhammad was both a prophet and a messenger. Prophets and messengers are considered to be divinely protected from sin, though still fully human and capable of all human states (eating, sleeping, and so on) that would not impede them in their mission.

3. The belief in the divinely revealed books: Muslims believe that Allah has revealed various books to messengers throughout time, including the Psalms to David, the Torah to Moses, the Evangel to Jesus, and the Qur'an to Muhammad. Because Muhammad is the last of the prophets, the Qur'an, as revealed to Muhammad, is considered protected for all time, whereas the previous revelations have been susceptible to alteration and therefore can only be read through the lens or criteria of the Qur'an.

4. The belief in the angels: Muslims believe that Allah has created sentient beings known as angels, which are made of light. They possess an ability to think and inquire, but they are not capable of disobeying the command of Allah. Therefore, there is no fallen angel in the Islamic tradition. Rather, the devil is from a species of creatures called jinn, who are made from smokeless fire and are capable of obedience

and disobedience, belief and disbelief. There are many different angels, although the most relevant to understanding Islam is Gabriel, the angel who delivered Allah's revelation to Muhammad.

5. The Day of Judgment: Muslims believe that Allah created the universe and its progression toward a definite end, in which all actions of humans and jinn will be weighed and judged, resulting in the eternal reward for the good believers, the temporary punishment of the bad believers, and the eternal punishment of the disbelievers. Disbelief entails learning and realizing the ultimate truths of Islam—especially Allah's oneness and the prophecy of Muhammad—and rejecting some or all of it.

6. Destiny: Muslims believe that whatever happens, whether sweet or bitter, occurs because of Allah's will. Human beings are accountable for the choices they make in life, yet all things happen because of Allah's will and power. Whatever hits wasn't meant to miss, and whatever misses wasn't meant to hit.

Since numbers 5 and 6 above deal with the concepts of death, the afterlife, and salvation, it is necessary to address some topics with which al-Ghazali assumes the reader is familiar. What follows is a brief summary of what has been mentioned in the Qur'an and hadith about death and the afterlife. After the life force leaves the body, there is a state called the interim world (*barzakh*). Your experience therein will be like either a pit of hell or a valley of paradise. The soul has some continued connection to the body in the grave, although the details are not clear. Two questioning angels will come to the deceased in the grave and ask a series of questions about your faith. This process will be easier for the believers and much harder for the hypocrites and disbelievers.

People are divided into three categories: believers, disbelievers, and those who will not be held accountable. A believer is a person who affirms the truths of the prophet sent to his or her time, place, and community. A disbeliever is a person who has heard an accurate representation of his or her prophet's message and rejects it in whole or in part. The third category of people, those who are not held accountable in the afterlife, are those who have not come of age (i.e., reached puberty or turned at least fifteen in the absence of puberty's onset), are not mentally competent (i.e., the insane or someone with a severe mental disability), or have not heard a complete and proper explanation of their prophet's teaching. Muslims believe that Muhammad was the final prophet for all times and places. From the perspective of interfaith dialogue, that means that Muslims believe the message the Prophet Muhammad came with is true and sufficient for all. There is no compulsion in religion; thus, people are free to accept or reject Islam. While Islam teaches that denial of Allah's message as revealed to the Prophet Muhammad, if accurately presented and understood, entails disbelief, the full definition of "denial" is known only to Allah. At what point a person reaches a level of knowledge and understanding of Islam that he or she is held accountable for not embracing it is known only by Allah. While on the one hand this is an exclusive claim to salvation for all who have heard, understood, and accepted the message of the prophet sent to their time (which includes past prophets and their communities), salvation, according to al-Ghazali, is widely inclusive of all those who have not actively and knowingly rejected Allah and His prophets. The oversimplified mentality of "we win, you lose" or "us versus them" is not intended by al-Ghazali. Rather, people are asked to reflect on Islam's claim that the singular, omnipotent, and omniscient Creator exists, is the only one worthy of worship, and has mercifully sent prophets with guidance. A person who has not received all the necessary facts through access to an accurate representation of prophetic guidance is not counted as a disbeliever.

This interim state (*barzakh*) continues until the Day of Resurrection, when all humans who ever existed are resurrected. Here begins the Day of Judgment, when all are judged for their deeds. It includes standing in queue, waiting for judgment, having your book of deeds handed to you, having your deeds weighed on a mighty scale, crossing over a bridge that leads to paradise (though some will not be able to cross and will tumble into hell), and so on. Heaven is described as an eternal abode in which there are lush gardens beneath which rivers flow. Its inhabitants never utter vain words and enjoy all sorts of pleasures, including fine food, clothes, castles, and company, as well as spiritual pleasures. The highest pleasure of heaven, as mentioned previously, is the vision of Allah, which occurs in a way that does not entail limitation or direction. Hell is described as an abode of pain and torment, temporary for the sinful believers, who eventually are granted amnesty and brought to heaven after "serving their time," and permanent for the disbelievers who rejected Allah and/or His prophets. The tortures of hell are harsh and many, though the worst of hell's tribulations is being cut off from witnessing Allah.

Death is a weighty matter, and the end point in the journey of life, after which your deeds come to an end. In Islam, there are no second chances after death; your record is sealed, and you are judged according to it.

The Dimension of *Ihsan* and the Perfection of Faith

The third dimension, *Ihsan*, is the perfection of faith, and the majority of al-Ghazali's *The Forty Foundations of Religion* is focused on it. This dimension is described by the Prophet Muhammad as worshipping Allah as though you see Him, and if you don't see Him, to know that He sees you. According to the Sufis, the mystics of Islam, these high states of perfected worship are achieved by purifying the soul of base traits such as lying, envy, pride, and arrogance and adorning the soul with meritorious traits such as patience, reliance on Allah, sincerity, and love of Allah. You worship Allah as though you see Him when your attachment to worldly things decreases, and your soul is drowned in the remembrance and spiritual witnessing of Allah. This witnessing, or spiritual knowledge of Allah, is called *ma'rifah*. If you have not achieved *ma'rifah*, then you strive to watch over your actions and inner states, knowing that Allah witnesses these actions at all times and places.

In addition to the purification of base traits and the adornment with commonly accepted meritorious states, there are a number of rare and lofty experiences that the Sufis discuss that might be classified as meritorious traits as well. Two experiences to which al-Ghazali often returns are the concepts of annihilation (*fana'*) and subsistence (*baqa'*). Al-Ghazali usually refers to *fana'* as a state in which you are annihilated of perception of any except Allah; even your own self disappears to you in this state, and all that remains is the spiritual perception of Allah. This state is not in and of itself the ideal and final state, as it is akin to losing consciousness. Rather, *fana'* is followed by *baqa'* (subsistence), which means that you are inwardly still focused on Allah but have "returned to your senses" and are able to interact with those around you and perform your religious and social duties.

Sufis, including al-Ghazali, often use other technical terms specific to their discipline such as *dhawq* (tasting), *wajd* (ecstasy), and *kashf* (unveiling), which refer to different experiences that occur as you decrease your connection to the physical and increase your connection to the spiritual. Not all Sufis use the same terminology, or if they use the same terminology, they do not always agree on the exact meaning of the term. For this reason, al-Ghazali and others stress that you should get to the intended meanings and not get caught up in the varying expressions of these meanings, because human language is insufficient for expressing matters of spirituality.

Some Sufis also talk about inner insinuations that occur in the heart of the person, calling him or her to lowly or noble attachments and states. Thus, a whole system of Sufi psychology emerges, which al-Ghazali discusses briefly in the *The Forty Foundations of Religion* and in more detail in *The Revival of the Religious Sciences*. Depending on your spiritual and psychological state, your perception of the world around you varies. If you are only connected to the physical, you will only perceive the physical world (*mulk*). However, as you decrease in physical attachments and increase in spiritual attachments, you will begin to have spiritual experiences, perceiving matters of the spiritual world (*malakut*). Beyond this, when you are fully immersed in loving remembrance and contemplation of the Divine, your perception becomes focused on the realm of the experience of the presence of the Divine (*jabarut*). Thus, although the world is one, it has three main aspects or dimensions, according to al-Ghazali, namely, the *mulk*, *malakut*, and *jabarut*.

Sufis differ in how they describe the levels of the soul and the corresponding aspects of the created universe. However, their core meanings tend to revolve around the agreed-upon elements of purification of base traits and adornment with meritorious traits, until your sole purpose and desire is to know, worship, and obey Allah. Although there are some necessary or interesting diversions into these topics in al-Ghazali's *The Forty Foundations of Religion*, from a practical standpoint, the primary emphasis is on purification and adornment.

The goals of purification of base traits and adornment with meritorious traits, the highest of which is experiential knowledge of Allah, are achieved by way of three main methods. The first is *dhikr*, meaning "remembrance of Allah." It can take on many forms, including chanting one or more of the ninety-nine names of Allah, reading the Qur'an, studying sacred knowledge, praying, reciting substantial litanies, or even singing and dancing. Sufis do not always agree on which forms of *dhikr* are the best or even necessary, but in general, the agreed-upon emphasis is on turning all of your attention to Allah at all times via remembrance of Him. *Dhikr* may be done in groups or alone, silently or aloud, again depending on the opinions and preferences of various Sufi masters.

The second method of achieving the goals of Sufism is called *mudhakarah*, which can be called the spiritual teachings of Sufism. This usually takes the form of the master-disciple relationship with a spiritual guide (*shaykh*, *murshid*, *pir*) and a spiritual aspirant (*murid*), that is, one who aspires to achieve the lofty states of Sufism. Sometimes these teachings are transmitted in daily, weekly, or occasional lectures, by way of one-on-one question-and-answer sessions, or even long distance through the exchange of letters. It is not just the sermonizing or assignment of specific spiritual exercises that makes *mudhakarah* a central component in the Sufi path, but also the transmission of the *hal*, or spiritual state, of the master to the disciple. Some Sufis have said witnessing the spiritual state of the master is better than a thousand sermons.

In addition to remembering Allah and the transmission of the spiritual teachings, the third core means of achieving the goals of Sufism is called *jihad al-nafs*, the struggle against the lower self. This can take on many forms, including committing yourself to reciting frequent and lengthy litanies, fasting often, living a frugal and simple lifestyle, and even avoiding permissible but unnecessary matters. It can also take on the form of spiritual exercises, such as refraining from the sins of the tongue (gossip, swearing) for a set period of time and instituting some sort of punitive measures for each failure. One example that I use in my university classes is to go twenty-four hours without backbiting, talebearing, or lying, and setting aside twenty-five cents for each failure as expiation. After a week or so of effort, students collect whatever money they have accrued in slipups and donate it to a charitable cause. The point of the struggle against the self is to discipline it, so that it decreases in its attachments to worldly matters and inclines toward the Divine.

The three dimensions of Islam and their associated sciences make up the body, mind, and soul of the faith. Another way of viewing this tripartite analysis is that they provide guidance for the core aspects of the worshipper, namely, the body, mind, and soul.

About the Translation

The book you have before you is an abridged translation of *The Forty Foundations of Religion*, with facing commentary. The book is divided into four sections: belief, practice, purification of the soul of base traits, and its adornment with meritorious traits. Book 1 is a short summary of Islamic belief. Book 2 is a summary of the most important ritual practices that lead to the end goals of Islamic spirituality, namely, experiential knowledge of Allah (gnosis). Book 3 deals with the base traits of which you must purify yourself in order to reach the ultimate spiritual realities to which Islamic belief and practice call you. Book 4 closes the work with a discussion of the meritorious spiritual and psychological traits and states that you must attain on your journey to Allah.

While translations of al-Ghazali's *The Revival of the Religious Sciences* and other similar texts abound, there are no translations—partial or complete—of *The Forty Foundations of Religion* available. Significantly shorter than *Revival*, al-Ghazali's *The Forty Foundations* provides the reader with a summarized and concise exposition of his spiritual world-view and methodology. Other translated works deal with some overlapping content, but I am not aware of a translated text in the English language that concisely covers the core points of al-Ghazali's Sufi thought and their relation to law and theology. It is hoped that this translation will be more accessible than some older translations of al-Ghazali's works and more concise than some of the more recent comprehensive translations. The commentary assumes little to no background knowledge and both explains the original text and introduces the reader to some of the ideas that al-Ghazali presumes the reader already knows.

The translation presented here is at times interpretive and other times literal. I have sought to strike a balance between the two, in hopes of expressing al-Ghazali's intent in the clearest possible form. Because this is an abridgment, I have used ellipses to indicate where certain passages have been omitted. Most often, ellipses represent the omission of large passages, though, at times, they represent the combining of shorter passages that form a summary of what has been omitted. Where ellipses would interrupt the flow, they were not included. I have summarized some of the omitted passages in the commentary, primarily in books 3 and 4. However, given the nature of an abridged translation, some gems may have been left out; their omission does not reflect a judgment of their worth, and it is hoped that a complete translation will one day surface.

It is customary to follow mention of Allah's name with "Exalted is He" or "Most High," or similar phrasing, as al-Ghazali does repeatedly in

The Forty Foundations. Likewise, it is customary for peace and blessings to be sought for the prophets, after mention of their names. Furthermore, after the mention of the Prophet Muhammad's family and companions, it is customary to say "May Allah be pleased with them." For those unfamiliar and unaccustomed to this convention, such interspersed praises and supplications can be distracting. It is with significant reservation that I omit all but the praises of Allah mentioned by al-Ghazali; the concerned reader, however, is requested to offer the omitted praises, blessings, and supplications, as he or she reads.

The Arabic edition of *The Forty Foundations of Religion* upon which this translation is based was published in 2003 by Dar al-Qalam, and edited by Abdullah A. H. Arawni. Arawni's edition includes the references for Qur'anic verses in brackets in the text. I have followed his example and left the bracketed Qur'anic citations in the main text, whereas al-Ghazali would likely not have included such references in the original, owing to the assumption that the reader would have memorized the Qur'an or significant amounts of it. An important contribution of Arawni's editorial work is his inclusion of the careful analysis of the hadiths cited by al-Ghazali, often relying on the work of the hadith scholar al-Iraqi (d. 1403), who undertook the painstaking task of checking every hadith narrated by al-Ghazali and finding its source, when available. Because al-Ghazali did not cite sources for hadiths, which he often paraphrased, or cited hadiths of dubious origin, I have endeavored to include only those hadiths whose origins could be traced to the recognized compendia of hadiths, with a few exceptions that are noted in the commentary.

A hadith is a transmitted saying, action, or tacit approval of the Prophet Muhammad. That is, someone either heard the Prophet say something, saw him do something, or saw someone do something in his presence that he did not oppose (i.e., he tacitly approved the action). Then the person who heard the statement or witnessed the action reported it to others. These reports were eventually collected by various scholars, who determined their authenticity based on their chains of narration, textual content, and other factors.

There are six main collections of hadith, listed below, that are commonly referred to and well known. They are often referred to as the "sound six." In addition to these six works, a number of other scholars compiled collections of hadith, some doing so before the "sound six" were compiled, and others significantly later. Although inclusion in any one of these collections does not automatically indicate its authenticity, those in the collections of the first two scholars (al-Bukhari and Muslim ibn Hajjaj) are almost universally accepted.

The compilers of the "sound six" are as follows:

Al-Bukhari (d. 870 CE)

Muslim ibn Hajjaj (d. 875 CE)

Al-Tirmidhi (d. 852 CE)

Ibn Majah (d. 886 CE)

Al-Nasa'i (d. 915 CE)

Abu Dawud (d. 888–89 CE)

Additional hadith narrators mentioned throughout *The Forty Foundations of Religion* include the following:

Ahmad ibn Hanbal (d. 855 CE)

Malik (d. 795 CE)

Al-Tabarani (d. 970–71 CE)

Al-Daylami (the father d. 1048 CE, the son d. 1090 CE)

Al-Bayhaqi (d. 1066 CE)

Ibn Hibban (d. 965 CE)

Ibn Mardawayh (d. 1019–20 CE)

Ibn Abi Dunya (d. 894 CE)

Al-Hakim (d. 1014 CE)

Thanks and Disclaimers

I would like to extend my sincere appreciation to Shaykh Faraz Rabbani for introducing this text to me and for providing me with his recorded oral translations for a few portions of book 1 and a significant amount of book 2. These helped set the tone for the rest of the translation and were very helpful in determining the meanings of some difficult passages. My own translations of these sections are very much indebted to Shaykh Faraz's translations. I have also benefitted from comparing my translations of sections from book 1 to Shaykh Nuh Keller's translations of similar portions from *The Revival of the Religious Sciences*. Where my translation differs, it is often due to slight differences of wordings in the two original texts (*Revival* and *The Forty Foundations of Religion*) or because certain terms or phrases fit more naturally with my own linguistic habits. Much of the commentary on books 3 and 4 reflect my studies of Shaykh Nuh Keller's writings and lectures, without which I would have little to no substantial knowledge of Sufism. I also thank Carl Sharif El-Tobgui for his assistance with a number of challenging passages in books 3 and 4. Finally, I would like to draw your attention to a rich and very useful website on al-Ghazali, which includes original Arabic texts as well as translations in English and other languages: www.Ghazali.org.

Al-Ghazali's intent in writing *The Forty Foundations of Religion* was to provide the reader with a comprehensive summary of some of the most important aspects of Islamic spirituality. It is not intended to be a do-it-yourself guide to spiritual enlightenment, as the spiritual path requires a solid foundation in the Islamic sciences and the guidance of a trained master. Though I am an avid student of the sacred sciences, I am not an authorized master of Sufism. Furthermore, although great effort has been made to properly reflect al-Ghazali's intent, there are inevitable subtleties that get lost in translation. With that, you are advised to treat the following pages as primarily informative and inspirational, rather than instructive. That is, there are suggestions in this text that could be spiritually, physically, or emotionally dangerous were they to be put into practice without consultation with an expert.

It is hoped that this abridged translation and commentary might add to the ever-growing corpus of translations and discussions of al-Ghazali's work and thought. Perfection is for Allah, so it is hoped that any short-comings might be overlooked. Should any errors be discovered, I would greatly appreciate their being brought to my attention.

Ghazali on the Principles
of Islamic Spirituality

1 "Allah" is a proper name designating the one true God of all. It is used by Arabic-speaking Jews, Christians, and Muslims much in the same way that English-speaking Jews, Christians, and Muslims use the name "God."

2 When writing a book, indeed with every good action, it is customary for Muslims to begin with the *Basmalah*, that is, saying, "In the name of Allah, the Compassionate, the Merciful."

3 Having preceded his introduction with the *Basmalah*, al-Ghazali proceeds with the *Hamdalah*, that is, saying, "All praise is due to Allah." Both conventions are in keeping with two different sayings attributed to the Prophet Muhammad: "All matters devoid of the *Basmalah* are cut off [from blessings]" and "All matters devoid of the *Hamdalah* are cut off [from blessings]." These have been narrated in the hadith collection of Abu Dawud and others.

4 Also customary is to follow the *Hamdalah* with the *Salawat*, that is, sending blessings on the Prophet Muhammad. The Prophet Muhammad was born in 570 CE and died in 633 CE. He lived in Arabia and was a merchant by trade. At forty years of age, he began experiencing what he and those around him believed to be revelations from Allah. Based on these revelations, known as the Qur'an, and the Prophet's explanation and demonstration of them, the religion of Islam as it is now known was born. However, it should be noted that while the laws and rituals may have changed throughout revelatory history, Muslims believe that the central message of Islam—submission to the one unique God (Allah)—is the same message sent to all prophets and messengers prior to Muhammad, including Adam, Moses, Abraham, Noah, and Jesus. By these standards, all previous prophets were Muslims, that is, those who submit to Allah.

☐ Al-Ghazali's Introduction

In the name of Allah,[1] the Compassionate, the Merciful.[2]

All praise is due to Allah,[3] Lord of the worlds. Peace and blessings be upon Muhammad[4] and his entire family.

5   *The Forty Foundations of Religion* is in fact an introduction to another al-Ghazali work titled *The Jewels of the Qur'an*, which has been translated into English. See *The Jewels of the Qur'an: Al-Ghazali's Theory* (London: Kegan Paul International, 1983).

6   The purpose of the work you have before you is to explain how the essential message of the Qur'an can be reflected upon and put into action.

7   In other words, the content of the verses that al-Ghazali discusses in *The Jewels of the Qur'an* deals with knowledge, outward actions, inward acts of purification, and inward acts of adornment. For this reason, *The Forty Foundations of Religion*, which serves as an introduction to *The Jewels of the Qur'an*, treats each of these four topics in separate sections, each composed of ten chapters. The knowledge of which he speaks is regarding Islam's primary theological beliefs and constitutes the first section of *The Forty Foundations of Religion*. The outward actions pertain to the rituals and observances of the person who practices Islam and is the subject matter of the second part of *The Forty Foundations of Religion*. The inward acts of purification relate to ridding yourself of base spiritual and psychological traits, such as pride, envy, and ostentation, and makes up the content of the third portion of *The Forty Foundations of Religion*. Finally, the inward acts of adornment refer to the meritorious states and traits with which you must adorn yourself, such as patience, reliance on Allah, and so on, and is the final section of *The Forty Foundations of Religion*.

8   That al-Ghazali considers the content of *The Forty Foundations of Religion* to be the "essence of the Qur'an" should not be taken lightly. One implication of this is that all other aspects of the faith and practice of Islam return to these foundational principles.

To begin: Perhaps you might say these Qur'anic verses that I narrate in *The Jewels of the Qur'an*[5] comprise different types of knowledge and works. You may ask whether or not it is possible to distinguish their purposes and to explain what they contain in a detailed manner. Likewise, [you may ask] is it possible to do so while showing you how to attain unto these Qur'anic verses in such a way that you can reflect on each one independently, knowing thereby the detailed description of the gates of felicity in both knowledge and action, in such a way that attaining unto its keys be facilitated for them through striving and reflection?[6]

I say, yes, that is possible, and indeed the aims of these Qur'anic verses can be divided into knowledge and action. Actions are divided into outward and inward, the latter being divisible into acts of purification and acts of adornment. These four divisions can be summarized as: knowledge, outward actions, blameworthy character traits of which one must purify oneself, and praiseworthy character traits with which one must adorn oneself.[7]

Each of these four divisions returns to ten foundational principles, thus the name of this book is *The Forty Foundations of Religion*. Whoever wishes to publish it independent of *The Jewels of the Qur'an* may do so; indeed it is the essence of the Qur'an.[8]

BOOK I
The Science of Belief

◇ In Islam there are six fundamental articles of faith. Although al-Ghazali does not focus on all six here in their entirety, they are part of what he assumes his reader knows. They are mentioned in greater detail in the introduction to this translation.

1   Allah is the One to whom the Muslim submits body and soul, dedicating inward and outward works and refining his or her conduct and character. Al-Ghazali therefore begins with a discussion of the entity of Allah, or Allah Himself, as the attributes of a being cannot be discussed without discussing the being itself.

2   Although it begins with "We say," al-Ghazali is the only author of this text. It is common in classical Arabic for an individual to speak in the first person plural form.

3   The term *'ibad* is often translated as both "worshippers" and "servants." It is the plural of the term *'abd*, which means "slave" or "servant." The worshipper of Allah is thereby a servant of Allah, the idea being that it is better to be a servant of Allah than a servant of your lower self.

4   The Qur'an is considered by Muslims to be the divinely revealed word of Allah. It was revealed to the Prophet Muhammad, but it was not the Prophet's words; rather, its words are from Allah. Other divinely revealed texts include the Torah as revealed to Moses, the Evangel as revealed to Jesus, and the Psalms as revealed to David. Muslims believe that Allah made Himself known to many in the generations prior to Muhammad by way of revealed books or prophets sent to reaffirm previous divinely revealed texts without being sent with texts of their own.

THE FIRST FOUNDATION

☐ Allah's Entity[1]

We say:[2] All praise is due to Allah, who made Himself known to His servants[3] by His revealed book (the Qur'an)[4] upon the tongue of His Prophet.

(conutinued on page 11)

5   Allah's Oneness is the primary theme of revelation; it is the essence of Islam and believed by Muslims to be the ultimate truth. From the affirmation of Allah's Oneness, all else follows. Muslim theologians argue that to negate Allah's beginningless eternality and endless eternality would lead to rational absurdities that ultimately negate His Oneness.

6   Allah's dissimilarity from His creation is a fundamental aspect of Islamic monotheism (*tawhid*).

7   The term *al-Samad* is difficult to translate. It implies eternality and independence. It also implies being depended upon, and therefore, in some translations of the *Surat al-Ikhlas*, chapter 112 of the Qur'an, it is translated as "the eternally besought." Allah is the One to whom all turn in need, who needs no one. The Prophet described *Surat al-Ikhlas* as being equivalent to one-third of the Qur'an; therefore, al-Ghazali is emphasizing the centrality of this chapter with regard to the proper belief in Allah.

8   With the term *al-Qayyum* (all-sustaining), al-Ghazali is alluding to another central Qur'anic description of Allah that is mentioned in "the verse of the throne" (*ayat al-kursi*) (2:255). Allah is described in this verse as *al-Qayyum*, the One who needs none to sustain Him and who sustains all things. The Prophet referred to "the verse of the throne" as the greatest single verse in the Qur'an because a central aspect of the prophetic message of Allah's Oneness is that Allah is the living and all-sustaining (*al-Hayy al-Qayyum*).

9   Al-Ghazali poetically uses a number of similar words and phrases to summarize the primary beliefs that Allah exists and is beginninglessly eternal, endlessly eternal, absolutely independent, dissimilar from His creation, and One in and of Himself, without partner or co-sharer in divinity. Later scholars have called these last five qualities "the attributes of negation," in that they negate all imperfections of Allah. Once you reflect on Allah's personal attribute (*sifat al-dhat*), namely the attribute of existence (*wujud*), you necessarily affirm the attributes of negation (*sifat al-salbiyyah*).

He made known that He is One in His Essence without partner,[5] singular without likeness to anything,[6] absolutely independent[7] with no opposite, solitary with no peer. He is beginninglessly pre-eternal with nothing before Him, unchanging and eternal with no beginning. His Existence endures with no terminus. He is perpetual, without end. He is all-sustaining,[8] with no cessation, everlasting, never passing. He was and shall remain characterized by all qualities of perfection. He does not come to an end with the passing of time. Indeed, He is the First, the Last, the Manifest, the Hidden, and He knows all things.[9]

10   Al-Ghazali is distinguishing Allah from atoms and bodies, the former being a philosophical term for the smallest, indivisible bits of matter, and the latter being made up of atoms. These terms are common in philosophy and theology, Muslim theologians having developed a unique theory of atomism in their theological discussions that took place in the first few centuries of Islam.

11   The terms "accident" and "accidental attributes" as used in philosophy and theology refer to attributes of a thing that come into existence and go out of existence. For example, a rock can be said to be moving at one moment and standing still at another. The attribute of movement is an accidental attribute whose existence ends with the existence of the accidental attribute of stillness. Allah, being eternal and dissimilar from His creation, does not undergo change, thus His attributes are not accidental attributes.

12   As mentioned in the Qur'an: "It was We who created man, and We know what dark suggestions his soul makes to him, for We are nearer to him than (his) jugular vein" (50:16).

THE SECOND FOUNDATION

☐ His Sacredness

He is not a body, possessing neither shape nor form. Nor is He an atom,[10] delimited in space and time. He does not resemble bodies, neither occupying space, nor being divisible. He is not an atom; they do not indwell in Him, nor does He indwell in them. Nor is He an accidental attribute;[11] they do not indwell in Him, nor does He indwell in them. He does not resemble anything, nor does anything resemble Him. There is nothing like unto Him, nor is He like unto anything. He is not limited by spatial extent, nor do the six directions surround Him. He is established over His throne in a way befitting His majesty, in a manner that He intended, transcendently beyond contact, fixedness, indwelling, or movement. The throne does not carry Him, rather the throne and its carriers are supported by the subtlety of His power; they are overwhelmed in His grasp. He is above the throne and above all things to the utmost limits, with an "aboveness" that does not increase His nearness to the throne or the sky. Rather He is the exalted in rank above the throne.

Despite that, He is close to all existent things,[12] closer to the servant than his carotid artery. And He witnesses all things, for His closeness does not resemble the closeness of bodies, just as His entity does not resemble the entities of bodies.

(conutinued on page 15)

13   Allah is not contained in time, and He is not affected by its passage.

14   Allah's attributes do not resemble human attributes. His power is infinite, timeless, unlimited, and independent, while human power is finite, in time, limited, and dependent on Allah.

15   Accidental properties such as motion and rest, hotness and coolness, and the like do not happen to Allah, as they are time-bound and need a cause to bring them into existence.

16   Witnessing Allah in paradise is considered the highest pleasure of paradise, greater than all the other sensual pleasures (such as fine food and clothes). It is therefore the completion or the apex of the enjoyment experienced in paradise. How this witnessing occurs is not known; however, it does not in any way entail limiting Allah to time or space.

He does not indwell in anything, nor does anything indwell in Him. Allah is exalted beyond being contained in a place, just as He is transcendently above being confined by time. Rather He was before He created time and space, and He is now as He has always been.[13]

His attributes do not resemble His creation.[14] He is transcendent beyond change and motion; created things do not indwell in Him, nor do accidental properties befall Him.[15] Rather, He remains with the qualities of His exaltedness, transcendent beyond extinction, and He remains in His attributes of perfection, free of needing any increase in perfection.

The Existence of His entity can be known to the intellect and witnessed by sight as a benevolent blessing for the virtuous in the abode of eternal dwelling and as completion of the blissful experiences [of the people of paradise] by beholding His noble countenance.[16]

17   Although Allah attributes to Himself the term *yad*, which is translated to mean "hand," it is not to be understood as a corporeal limb. You cannot understand modality, or how-ness (*kayfiyyah*), with regard to Allah, yet you can understand how you are in relation to Allah, namely, entirely under His power and command.

18   Nothing of the created universe exists except that it was created by Allah. From the most distant supernova to the wing of a gnat, it is all under the power and command of Allah.

19   This is a reference to one of Islam's core articles of faith, namely, belief in destiny. Human actions are created by Allah, despite humans choosing them. Therefore, although Allah's power brings about fire when a burning match meets with a ball of cotton, you would be held accountable for choosing to put fire to cotton if a negative impact were to arise from its burning. This is called the theory of acquisition (*kasb*). You acquire reward or punishment for the actions you choose, but the actual effect is brought into existence by Allah's power.

THE THIRD FOUNDATION

☐ Allah's Omnipotent Power

He is living, powerful, overwhelming, and overpowering. He is unaffected by inability or incapacity. He is not overcome by slumber or sleep, nor is He attributed with annihilation or death. He possesses sovereignty, dominion, might, and force. His is the power, authority, and vanquishing, as well as the creation and command. Enfolded in His right hand[17] are the heavens, and all created things are overwhelmed in His grasp.

He is alone in creating, bringing into being and fashioning all things from nonexistence.[18] He creates all things and their actions and appoints their provisions and life spans.[19] Nothing escapes His grasp, and nothing is beyond His power in the disposal of matters. The things He can do are innumerable, and the matters that He knows are endless.

20   Allah, being transcendently beyond time and space, knows with an eternal and unchanging knowledge, rather than by way of acquired and imparted knowledge. In other words, Allah's knowledge does not increase and decrease. He knows all that is, that is not, or that will or will not come into existence.

☐ Allah's Omniscient Knowledge

He knows all things knowable, encompassing all that occurs in the depths of the earths to the highest heavens. Nothing escapes His knowledge, not even an atom's weight in the earth nor in the sky. Rather, He knows the steps of a black ant on a black stone in the dark night, and He perceives the movement of a dust particle on a windy day. He knows that which is secret and that which is more concealed ... with knowledge that is beginninglessly eternal....[20]

21   *Al-Mubdi'* and *al-Mu'id*, the Originator and the Returner, are two of the ninety-nine names of Allah.

22   In the Islamic tradition, the jinn (genies) are sentient beings made of smokeless fire. Like human beings, they can be either good or bad, owing to their possessing consciousness and the ability to choose their actions. In their natural form, they are invisible to human beings; however, they can take on the shape of human beings or animals and thereby be seen.

23   Angels are sentient beings made of light. Unlike the jinn, they do not possess will over their actions. Rather, they are in constant obedience to Allah's command. Thus, there are no fallen angels in the Islamic tradition.

24   In the Islamic tradition, devils (*shayatin*) are usually evil jinn, such as Iblis, the devil himself. However, evil human beings are also referred to as devils, so this could be read as referring to all evil humans and jinn.

25   Allah's will, like His power and knowledge, are absolute and eternal attributes, which do not come into or go out of existence. He was thus ever willing, even "before" He created the universe.

THE FIFTH FOUNDATION

☐ Allah's Will

He wills all existent things, directing all that occurs. Nothing transpires in the physical or spiritual worlds, whether it be little or much, small or large, good or bad, beneficial or harmful, belief or disbelief, knowledge or ignorance, victory or loss, increase or decrease, obedience or disobedience, except by His decree, destining, wisdom, and willing. For whatever He wills is, and whatever He does not will is not.

Neither peripheral glance nor thought escapes His will; rather He is the Originator and the Returner,[21] doer of whatever He wills. None can repel His command nor repeal His destiny. There is no escape for His servant from disobeying Him, except by His divinely granted success and mercy, and no power to obey Him, except by His help and will. If all humans, jinn,[22] angels,[23] and devils[24] were to gather together to move or still even a particle in the universe without His willing and choosing it, they would be incapable of doing so.

His will is established in His entity, along with His other attributes, and with that, He is ever described by the attribute of will.[25] He willed from timeless pre-eternity the existence of all things in the times that He destined for them, and they occurred, neither before nor after, in the times that He willed from timeless pre-eternity. Rather, they occurred according to His knowledge and will, without substitution or change.

(continued on page 23)

26   Al-Ghazali is further emphasizing Allah's timeless eternality. Allah's will is not a succession of thoughts and inclinations, as is our own; rather, it is timelessly eternal and thus is not dependent on anything else. Furthermore, being timelessly eternal, Allah is not busied with one matter to the exclusion of another.

27   Returning again to the subject of destiny, the upshot is that whatever exists in the created universe is inescapably connected to Allah's will, power, and knowledge. Since the subject of the relationship between accountability for your actions and Allah's omnipotence entails some intellectual complexities, many have slipped on this issue. Omitted here, the next passage is where al-Ghazali turns his attention to some of the sects of Islam whose views on free will and destiny were considered heretical. According to the mainstream perspective on the matter, you are not forced to choose your actions and are therefore accountable for your choices. However, you are not in and of yourself capable of bringing the effects of your actions, as Allah creates all causes and effects.

He directs matters without consecutive thoughts, nor awaiting the passage of time. With that, nothing busies Him from anything else.[26] Glorified and exalted is He....

Many a foot has slipped on this issue.... With that, everything that happens in the universe ... is not excluded from Allah's will....[27]

28   While the human being should be constantly aware of Allah's hearing and seeing all human thoughts and actions, these actions are not perceived in the same way that created beings perceive them. Allah is not dependent on an eardrum with which to register sound waves, or a pupil to permit light into an eyeball to be projected onto a retina and translated into an image. Rather, Allah's capacities for hearing and seeing are not understood by the finite mind.

THE SIXTH FOUNDATION

□ Allah's Hearing and Seeing

He hears and sees all. No sound escapes His hearing, no matter how concealed. No sight escapes His vision, no matter how small. No distance obscures His hearing, nor does darkness impede His vision. He sees without pupil or eyelid, and hears without ear canal or ears, just as He knows without a heart, strikes without a limb, and creates without instruments. His attributes do not resemble the attributes of created things; likewise His entity does not resemble the entity of created things.[28]

29 The speech of Allah is not like the speech of created beings. It does not refer to a sound produced by the vibration of vocal chords and subsequent sound waves moving through air particles. The Qur'an is called "Allah's speech," both in the sense that it was not composed by someone else (such as the Prophet) and in that it points to Allah's eternal attribute of speech. This matter is a slippery theological discussion, over which much ink has been spilled and much disagreement has arisen. The main point is that the Qur'an and the other books of divine revelation are lofty and noble communications directly from the creator and sustainer of the universe.

THE SEVENTH FOUNDATION

☐ Allah's Speech

He speaks, commands, forbids, promises, and threatens with beginninglessly eternal speech that is established in His entity. His speech does not resemble the speech of created things, just as His entity does not resemble the entities of created things. His speech is not a sound generated by way of air or the colliding of bodies, nor is it a letter[29] articulated through the compression of the lips or moving the tongue.

The Qur'an, the Torah, the Evangel, and the Psalms are His books, revealed to His messengers. The Qur'an is recited by tongues, written in books, and memorized in hearts, though it is beginninglessly eternal and established in the entity of Allah Most High. It is not dissevered or separated by being transmitted to hearts and pages.

Moses (peace be upon him) heard the speech of Allah without sound or letter, just as the righteous see the entity of Allah—glorified is He—in the afterlife without substance, form, color, or accident. Since He [Allah] has these previously mentioned attributes, He is living, knowing, powerful, willing, hearing, seeing, and speaking, by way of life, knowledge, power, will, hearing, seeing, and speech, not merely by way of His entity.

30 This statement is mistakenly considered by some writers on Sufism to have been reported by the Prophet Muhammad. Despite the statement not being traceable to the Prophet, its meaning is considered true, that is, that Allah created the universe and all its inhabitants in order to know and worship Him.

31 This returns to what was previously mentioned of Allah's being able to choose between creation of the universe and leaving it in nonexistence.

32 Were another human being to cause a fellow human being to suffer such things, it would be oppression, for it is not the right of one to cause pain to another. However, Allah owns all of creation, and it is His to do with as He chooses. In His wisdom, He causes some to suffer and others to experience pleasure. All experiences have a wisdom embedded, from which you can seek your ultimate role and goal in life.

THE EIGHTH FOUNDATION

☐ His Actions

There is nothing in existence other than Him, except that it is created by His action, flowing from His justice in the best, most perfect, complete, and just way. He is wise in His actions and just in His rulings. His justice is not analogous to the justice of His servants, since one conceives of the injustice of a servant with regard to his dealing with what another possesses. It is inconceivable that injustice be attributable to Allah Most High—glorified is He—since none but Allah can be found to have true possession of anything such that He could deal unjustly with it.

All besides Him—whether human or jinn, devil or angel, sky or earth, animal or vegetable, composite body or accident, perceived or sensed—was brought into existence, created by His power after not existing, after there being nothing. He alone existed in timeless pre-eternity, and there was nothing besides Him. He originated creation, manifesting His power, actualizing His will, and realizing His eternal word. As the saying goes, "I was a hidden treasure and desired to be known."[30] His bringing creation into being was not due to needing anything from it.

Creation, origination, and charging humans and jinn with responsibilities were out of His pure generosity, not of necessity, and blessings and bestowals are of His benevolence, not of obligation.[31] From Him stems generosity and goodness, blessings and munificence. He is capable of imposing on His servants all kinds of tribulations and afflicting them with all sorts of suffering and enduring of illnesses. Were He to do that, it would be just, and not evil or oppressive.[32]

(coninued on page 31)

33   According to al-Ghazali and other scholars of the Ash'ari school of
Sunni theology, the human mind cannot determine with absolute
accuracy and certainty which actions are beneficial and which are
harmful. Indeed, one action may cause immediate pleasure but greater
harm later, while another action may result in the opposite. The effects
of some actions may not ever be apparent, whereas a given effect may
be attributed erroneously to an apparent cause. Painful experiences
sometimes lead to pleasure, and vice versa. Thus, the good and the
bad, the commanded and the prohibited are only known by way of
Allah's messengers. Other scholars, such as the followers of the
Maturidi school of Sunni theology, however, felt that the intellect
could, in fact, determine the wisdom and ruling for an action.

He rewards His servants for their acts of obedience by virtue of His generosity and justice, not because of their worthiness or due to obligation. He is not obligated to do anything, oppression is inconceivable from Him, and He does not owe anything to anyone. Acts of obedience are an obligation for His servants by way of His having informed them on the tongues of His messengers, not merely by the intellect alone.[33] He sent messengers, making known their truthfulness with manifest miracles. They transmitted His commands and prohibitions, promises and warnings, and He made belief in that with which they came obligatory for His servants.

[34]   The legally responsible person, or, more literally, the one charged with a duty (*mukallaf*), is a person who (a) is sane, (b) is of age (having reached puberty or at least age fifteen), and (c) has accurately heard the message of the Prophet Muhammad without alteration or omission. A person who lacks one or more of these three characteristics is not held accountable on the Day of Judgment, as stated in the Qur'an: "Who receiveth guidance, receiveth it for his own benefit: who goeth astray doth so to his own loss: No bearer of burdens can bear the burden of another: nor would We visit with Our Wrath until We had sent an apostle (to give warning)" (17:15).

[35]   The word "scale" is a literal translation of *mizan*, which has a broader meaning, as the next passage indicates, of being a tool of measurement.

[36]   The Bridge (*as-Sirat*), as al-Ghazali explains, is a bridge that passes over hell. All human beings will have to pass over this bridge in order to get to heaven. For some, it will be an easy pass, as though it were a wide road. For others, it will be a treacherous path, as though walking over a thin hair as sharp as a sword. For others, they may not succeed in passing and will fall from it into hell. It is a fundamental aspect of Islamic faith, according to al-Ghazali, and is mentioned explicitly in many hadiths, as well as, according to some interpretations, in the Qur'an.

THE NINTH FOUNDATION

□ The Last Day

Allah Most High separates bodies and souls at death, then He reunites them on the Day of Judgment, and resurrects those in their graves, and brings forth that which was in their hearts. Every responsible person[34] will plainly see what he or she has done, the good and the evil of it, finding the trivial and the conspicuous recorded in a book. Neither the great nor the small deed will be left out, except that it is enumerated therein. Everyone will have the measure of their actions made known, the good and the bad, by a just standard against which they will be weighed on a scale.[35] The scale of deeds is not equivalent to a scale that weighs objects, just as the astrolabe, which measures points in time, is not equivalent to the ruler, which measures spaces.

Then they are taken to account for their deeds, speech, secrets, innermost thoughts, intentions, and beliefs, those that they disclosed and those that they hid. They differ with regard to their reckoning; some will be interrogated, some forgiven, while others will enter heaven without being called to account.

They are sent over the Bridge,[36] which is a bridge spanning the abode of the wretched and the abode of the felicitous. It is sharper than a sword and thinner than a hair. Those who were established on the straight path in this life will hasten across it, commensurate with their deeds, while those who deviated from the straight path will be made to stumble and creep along, except those who are generously spared.

(continued on page 35)

37   What is implied here by "as a delegation" is that the people of felicity—those who will be saved and therefore happy in the afterlife—will be led just as an honored delegation is led to the king.

38   Those with an atom's weight of faith will eventually be removed from the fire, but not until they have "burned off" their sins, that is, of course, unless Allah forgives them and commutes their punishment.

39   There are many types of intercession. Some may intercede on another's behalf, thereby sparing them of any punishment. Others will intercede to shorten another's punishment. Additionally, one may intercede and raise another's rank in paradise. Of all the forms of intercession, the intercession of the prophets will be the most far-reaching.

40   As mentioned elsewhere, witnessing Allah in paradise is not in the sense of your seeing a physical object, as Allah is not bound by time, space, or anything of His creation.

They will also be questioned, and Allah will question whomever He wills from among the prophets regarding their conveying the message. He will also ask whomever He wills from among the disbelievers regarding their denying the messengers and from among those who innovated and deviated from the example of the Prophet Muhammad. Whomever He wills from among the Muslims will be asked about their deeds, and those truthful and faithful ones whom He wills will be asked about their faithfulness. He will ask whomever He wills from among hypocrites about their hypocrisy.

Then the felicitous will be led to the Most Merciful as a delegation,[37] and the evildoers will be led to hell. Then He will command that the monotheists be removed from the fire after their retribution[38] until there remains in the fire not one in whose heart is an atom's weight of faith. Some will be removed before the completion of their punishment and retribution by way of the intercession of the prophets, the scholars, the martyrs, and whoever has the station of intercession.[39]

Then the people of felicity will abide in heaven eternally, living a luxurious and blessed life and gazing at the countenance of Allah Most High.[40] The people of wretchedness will abide in the fire constantly under all sorts of punishments, prevented by a veil from gazing at the countenance of Allah, possessor of majesty and honor.

41   Miracles are preternatural events, that is, breaks in the normal links of causality. A prophetic miracle (*mu'jizah*) is such a break in causality, accompanied by a challenge. Similar events, called marvels (*karamah*), can happen at the hands of pious people though they are neither accompanied by a challenge nor occur on cue.

42   There are different types of inspiration. Prophetic inspiration or revelation (*wahy*) is specific to prophets and has come to an end with the death of the Prophet Muhammad. Inspiration that occurs to people who are not prophets (*ilham*) and true dreams can happen to anyone at any time, though these are not dependable enough to be relied upon.

43   Revelation is usually delivered by the angel Gabriel to those whom Allah has singled out for the office of prophecy. In the case of Moses, the Qur'an narrates his experience of hearing Allah's speech directly without intermediary.

44   The law given to Muhammad repeals the laws given to previous prophets.

45   The sacred law, or shariah, is the law as revealed to Muhammad by Allah. It encompasses everything from proper bathing to how to run an empire, and everything in between. Some prophets have been sent with differing shariahs, while others were sent to reestablish those of a previous prophet. Some received rules and regulations solely for their time and place, while in the case of Muhammad, his law is generally universal, for all time. Some rules and regulations, however, were specific to Muhammad's personal practice. Although there are certain commands and prohibitions shared by all, there are also changes to the law that occurred from one prophet to the next. The shariah of Moses, for example, prohibited working on the Sabbath, whereas the shariah of Muhammad abrogated that prohibition and permitted working on the Sabbath.

46   Belief in Allah is not sufficient without the affirmation of His messengers. See Introduction, page xxi.

THE TENTH FOUNDATION

☐ Prophecy

Allah created the angels and sent the prophets, confirming them with miracles.[41] All of the angels are Allah's servants. Allah Most High says in the Qur'an, "They celebrate His praises night and day, nor do they ever flag or intermit" [21:19–20]. The prophets are sent as messengers to His creation. Divine inspiration[42] came to the prophets by way of angels.[43] The prophets speak from inspiration, not from caprice.

Allah sent Muhammad—the unlettered Prophet from the tribe of the Quraysh—with His message to the entirety of Arabs and non-Arabs, jinn and humans, thereby abrogating[44] with the sacred law[45] of Muhammad those laws that came before. Allah made Muhammad the Master of Humanity and made the testification of faith in his prophecy a condition for the completeness of your faith.[46] The testification of faith in Muhammad's prophecy is "Muhammad is the messenger of Allah."

Allah obligated humans and jinn to believe in the entirety of what the prophets reported to them regarding matters of this world and the next and enjoined them to follow the Prophet in emulation of his example.

Allah said in the Qur'an, "... So take what the Messenger assigns to you, and deny yourselves that which he withholds from you. And fear Allah. For Allah is strict in punishment" [59:7].

(continued on page 39)

47   Whatever will draw you nearer to Allah has been commanded and facilitated for you.

48   According to al-Ghazali and other scholars, the unaided intellect is incapable of determining with certainty whether or not a given action is good or bad. Rather, Allah reveals the prohibitions to humanity via words of prophets.

49   The ninety-nine names of Allah (*al-asma' al-husna*) include the Compassionate, the Merciful, the Protector, the Creator, and so on. See al-Ghazali's "The Ninety-Nine Beautiful Names of Allah" in *The Jewels of the Qur'an: Al-Ghazali's Theory* (London: Kegan Paul International, 1983).

50   There is often confusion over the difference between divine names and attributes. The divine names are derived from the attributes, such that the One who possesses power is called the Powerful, while other names are derived from multiple attributes.

51   It is a common Islamic convention to end a book, chapter, lesson, meeting, or any noble activity with similar expressions.

52   In the remaining paragraphs that have been left untranslated, al-Ghazali goes on to explain two levels of belief associated with the beliefs mentioned in this section. The first level is knowledge of the rational and textual proofs for these beliefs, without knowing their inner secrets. These are mentioned in a section on belief in *The Revival of the Religious Sciences* and in his book titled *Middle Way in Belief*. The second level, which is superior to the first, is knowledge of their inner secrets, their subtle meanings, and the reality of their outer meanings.

Nothing that draws people nearer to Allah—glorified and exalted is He—has been omitted; He commands them to do it, leading them to its path.[47] Nothing draws nearer to the hellfire, distancing them from Allah Most High, except that He prohibited them from it, making known its path. Indeed, one is not guided to these matters [of commands and prohibitions] by the unaided intellect, opinion, or intelligence; rather they are secrets from paradise disclosed to the hearts of the prophets.[48]

All praise is due to Allah for that to which He guided and for making known His beautiful names[49] and exalted attributes.[50] Peace and blessings be upon Muhammad the Chosen, the Seal of the Messengers, and upon his family and companions.[51]

□ Conclusion

This completes the section that seeks to explain the reality of the Islamic creed. Know that what we have mentioned therein is the upshot of the sciences of the Qur'an, gathering together whatever is connected to belief in Allah, His messengers, and the Last Day. It is an interpretation of the beliefs that the hearts of every Muslim necessarily encompass, such that he or she believes with full conviction.[52]

BOOK II
Outward Actions

✧ Book 2 deals with *Islam*, or the submission of your actions to Allah's command, and includes Islam's five foundational matters of ritual and practice: (1) testification of faith (*shahadah*), (2) the five daily ritual prayers (*salah*), (3) fasting in the month of Ramadan, (4) giving a set percentage of your stored wealth to the poor and needy (*zakah*), and (5) the once-in-a-lifetime pilgrimage to Mecca (the Hajj). In addition to four of the five pillars of *Islam* (all but the testification of faith), al-Ghazali also treats the topics of Qur'anic recitation, remembrance of Allah (the meditative recitation of prayers, litanies of Qur'anic verses, and/or the names of Allah), and other actions that affect a person's spiritual journey.

1 The term "prayer" (*al-salah*) throughout this section refers to ritual prayer, which consists of specific movements, supplications, and Qur'anic recitations. The term "supplication" (*al-du'a*) refers to the more general act of asking something of Allah without the set movements, recitations, and other conditions of ritual prayer.

2 This statement of the Prophet Muhammad, called a hadith, is narrated in the hadith collection of al-Bayhaqi (d. 1066 CE), an eleventh-century Sunni hadith expert. The attribution of this statement to the Prophet is not absolutely verifiable, yet its text is permissible to narrate, as its meaning is consistent with other verifiable texts. In the terminology of the hadith scholars, its chain of narration is weak.

3 The command is not merely to pray, but to establish ritual prayer in your daily life as a means of remembering and being close to Allah throughout the day. If you absentmindedly miss your ritual prayer at its prescribed time and then later realize that the time has passed and you did not do the prayer, then you must make it up upon remembering it. I understand al-Ghazali's statement "He does not merely say, 'Pray!'" to indicate that a concerted and intentional effort to have the day punctuated by prayer at the prescribed times is necessary.

THE FIRST FOUNDATION

☐ Ritual Prayer[1]

Allah Most High said in the Qur'an, "And establish the ritual prayer for My remembrance" [20:14].

The Prophet is reported to have said, "The prayer is the foundation of religion."[2]

Know that in your prayer, you are intimately calling upon your Lord. So look to how you pray, and guard therein three matters so that you might be counted among those who guard and properly establish their prayers. For Allah has only ordered the *establishment* of prayer, saying, "And establish the prayer" [20:14]. He does not merely say, "Pray!"[3]

Allah praises those who carefully guard the prayers, saying, "And this is a Book that We have sent down, bringing blessings, and confirming (the revelations) that came before it, that thou mayest warn the mother of cities and all around her. Those who believe in the hereafter believe in this (Book), and they are constant in guarding their prayers" [6:92].

(continued on page 45)

4   The obligatory ablutions before prayer consist *at minimum* of washing your face; washing right hand and arm up to and including the elbow, and then the left hand and arm; wiping your head; and washing your right foot up to and including the ankle, and then the left foot. These actions are preceded by the intention to perform the obligatory ablutions and are done in the order mentioned here. They must be performed before commencing prayer, and they need not be renewed at the next prayer time unless you have experienced a state of minor ritual impurity—such as having fallen asleep or having passed anything from your private parts, such as urine, gas, or stool—or experienced a state of major ritual impurity, which necessitates the more comprehensive purificatory bath (*ghusl*). Major ritual impurity includes having sexual intercourse, ejaculating, or experiencing menstrual or postnatal bleeding. The purificatory bath can take the form of washing the hands, rinsing the mouth, snuffing water into your nose and blowing it out, then the ablutions described above, finally followed by washing the rest of the body. For more details, see *Imam Nawawi's Manual of Islam* (Evanston, IL.: Sunna Books, 1994).

5   *Sunan* (sing. *sunnah*) literally means "ways" or "paths," denoting a well-trodden path. The prophetic *sunan* with regard to the ritual ablutions are those that the Prophet Muhammad did himself and highly recommended that others do so as well. In this case, al-Ghazali is referring to ablutions beyond the obligatory: saying *Basmalah*, washing your hands three times, brushing your teeth with a toothstick (*miswak*) or toothbrush, rinsing your mouth three times, snuffing water into your nose and blowing it out three times, washing your face and arms three times, wiping your head once, rinsing your ears three times, and washing your feet three times.

6   There is a remembrance or supplication associated with each aspect of the ablutions.

7   Literally, *al-waswas* means "whisperings" and in this context refers to the whisperings or suggestions of the devil that cause a person to have misgivings or doubts.

Those who carefully guard their prayers are of three types:

1. The first is the one who carefully guards his ritual purity by performing a thorough and proper ablution[4] before prayer, meaning that he adheres to all the prophetic ways[5] and statements of remembrance[6] that have been transmitted with regard to each aspect. Such a person cautiously guards the purification of his clothes and body as well, and in all cases does so with a caution that does not open the door to neurotic misgivings.[7] The devil strives to open this door to waste time such that you spend more time doing ablutions than the act of worship itself.

   Know that the meaning of purity of clothes is the outer shell, purity of body is the inner shell, while purity of the heart is the inner core. The purification of the heart from reprehensible character traits is the most important of the three necessary types of purification; however, outward purification impacts the shining of spiritual light upon the heart. If you perform your ritual ablution thoroughly and completely, such that you feel outward cleanliness, you will also find in your heart an inward spiritual expansion and serenity, due to the spiritual secret found in the relationship between the outward world and the higher spiritual worlds.

   If you do not find after your purification and thorough ritual ablution anything of spiritual serenity, then know that the dirt that has affected your heart from the muddy dross of worldly desire and your busying yourself with it has resulted in weakening your heart's capacity to discern spiritual subtleties. So busy yourself with polishing and purifying your heart, for this is more essential for you than anything else in which you may be presently engaged.

(continued on page 47)

8   Just as the actions of ablutions have remembrances and recommended acts associated with them, so too does each aspect of the ritual prayer. See al-Ghazali's "Beginning of Guidance," available in its entirety at www.Ghazali.org/books/m_quasem-79.pdf.

9   Al-Ghazali uses the comparison to animals in that they have an outward form as well as an inward reality, namely a soul. He then goes on to discuss the outward and inward components of prayer.

10   The integrals (*arkan*) are those necessary components of ritual prayer whose omission would render the entire prayer null and void.

11   These are the nonessential components of ritual prayer (*ab'ad*), translated literally as "parts of a thing," whose inclusion increases the merit of prayer but whose omission does not affect its validity.

12   This is in reference to the pronouncement "*Allahu Akbar*" ("Allah is great"), which opens prayer and precedes most of the major movements within prayer.

13   This refers to an opening supplication, which begins with "I turn my face toward the One who originated the heavens and earth as a pure monotheist, one who submits...." See *Imam Nawawi's Manual of Islam* (Evanston, IL.: Sunna Books, 1994).

2. The second type of those who carefully guard their prayers are those who hold fast to the prophetic ways related to prayer and its outward actions and verbal remembrances and glorifications of Allah,[8] for each has a spiritual secret and effect on the heart.

   Know that the prayer has a form that the Lord of all lords has fashioned for it, just as He gave a form to the animals.[9] The soul of prayer is intention, sincerity, and presence of heart. Its body consists of the outward actions. Its essential limbs are the integrals,[10] and its nonessential limbs are the recommended actions....[11] Know that the root of the prayer is exaltation and reverence; these qualities are contravened by carelessness with regard to the proper manners and etiquette of the prayer.

3. The third type of person who carefully guards his prayers is one who carefully guards the soul of prayer. Sincerity and presence of heart in all parts of the prayer and the characterizing of the heart at each moment with the meanings of the prayer are what is meant by "the soul of the prayer." So do not prostrate nor bow except that your heart is reverent and humbled in accordance with what is expressed with your outward movements, for what is sought is the submission of the heart, not the submission of the body.

Do not say, "Allah is great,"[12] while your heart holds something to be greater than Allah. Do not say, "I have directed my heart,"[13] except that your heart is, in every regard, entirely directed toward Allah, and completely turned away from all else.

(continued on page 49)

14   This refers to the first verse of the opening chapter of the Qur'an, which is as follows:

> *In the name of Allah, Most Gracious, Most Merciful.*
>
> *1. Praise be to Allah, the Cherisher and Sustainer of the worlds;*
>
> *2. Most Gracious, Most Merciful;*
>
> *3. Master of the Day of Judgment.*
>
> *4. Thee do we worship, and Thine aid we seek.*
>
> *5. Show us the straight way,*
>
> *6. The way of those on whom Thou hast bestowed Thy Grace,*
>
> *7. Those whose (portion) is not wrath, and who go not astray.*

15   Al-Ghazali uses the term *jahada*, meaning "to strive" or "to exert." It is the same term from which the controversial term *jihad* is derived, indicating that this term is used primarily with regard to an inner spiritual struggle and secondarily with regard to a defensive physical struggle. The latter usage nonetheless has nothing to do with terrorism or targeting noncombatants, which are rejected by Islam.

Do not say, "All praise is due to Allah,"[14] except that your heart is overflowing with thankfulness for Allah's blessings upon you, rejoicing in them joyously. Do not say, "You alone we worship," except that you truly feel your weakness and incapacity, and that neither you nor anyone else besides Him has any power. Likewise, [connect your heart to] all the acts of remembrance and actions within the prayer. The explanation of this is lengthy and we have explained it in detail in *The Revival of the Religious Sciences*. So exert[15] yourself such that you bring your heart back to the prayer, in order that you are not heedless in it from beginning to end; for a person only gets from his prayer that of which he was conscious. If you find it difficult to have presence of heart in your prayer, then to the extent of your heedlessness, increase in your superogatory prayers until your heart becomes present.

16   There are two terms used here, *zakah* and *sadaqah*. The former refers to the mandatory 2.5 percent poor tax that each Muslim must pay from his or her stored wealth over the course of a full lunar year, providing your savings do not dip below the minimum threshold (*nisab*) at any point throughout the year. Thus, if you save $1,000 in a given year, you pay $25 in *zakah* that year. It is not technically charity, as that money is actually considered to belong to the poor and other deserving recipients. *Sadaqah*, on the other hand, refers to voluntary charity from personal wealth, which can be of any amount, at any time.

17   Narrated in the hadith collection of Ahmad ibn Hanbal, a ninth-century jurist and hadith scholar, whose school of law—the Hanbali school—is one of the four main schools of Sunni law. "Like this and like this" refers to the gestures of the Prophet Muhammad, who demonstrated as he spoke, the meaning being that you give generously.

18   "Moral responsibility" (*taklif*) means that you are held responsible for what you believe and do. In Islam, those who are responsible for their beliefs and actions are held accountable in this life and in the next. The conditions of *taklif*, as mentioned previously, are generally that you are an adult (having reached puberty or at least age fifteen), are sane, and have accurately heard the message of the Prophet without alteration or omission.

THE SECOND FOUNDATION

☐ Poor Tax and Charity[16]

Allah Most High says, "The parable of those who spend their substance in the way of Allah is that of a grain of corn: it groweth seven ears, and each ear hath a hundred grains. Allah giveth manifold increase to whom He pleaseth; and Allah careth for all and He knoweth all things" [2:261].

The Prophet said, "Most people are destroyed except those who give like this and like this."[17]

Know that spending your wealth in the ways of good is one of the integrals of religion. The secret of being charged with moral responsibility[18] with regard to your wealth is for numerous reasons, namely, the many benefits connected with it that are advantageous to people and societies, as well as the fulfillment of needs and hardships.

Money is beloved by people, yet they are commanded to love Allah. They claim this love of Allah through faith itself, so Allah has made spending of one's wealth an indicator of his or her love and a test of the trueness of his or her claim to love Him, for all things that are beloved to people are spent for the greatest thing that the heart loves.

(continued on page 53)

19   Abu Bakr al-Siddiq was a very important companion of the Prophet
Muhammad. After the Prophet's death, he became the first caliph, or
ruler, over the Muslim community.

With regard to spending their wealth, there are three levels of people:

1. The first are the strongest, namely, those who spend all that they possess, spending nothing for themselves; these are the truest in their covenant to love Allah. This was done by Abu Bakr al-Siddiq,[19] for when he came to give all his wealth in charity, the Prophet asked, "What have you kept for yourself?" Abu Bakr replied, "Allah and His messenger."

2. The second type of people with regard to spending are the intermediate level, namely, those who were not able to lift their hand from their wealth all at once. However, they held on to their wealth not merely for worldly enjoyment, but rather to spend it on the needy who might later appear. They are content for themselves with that which gives them strength to worship. If a person in need appears to them, they hasten to fulfill their need and ease their hardship. They do not limit themselves merely to the obligatory minimum of the poor tax; rather, their main goal in holding on to their wealth is to fulfill any needs that may appear.

3. The third type of people with regard to spending consist of those who are weak. They merely give the obligatory minimum, neither more nor less.

These are the three levels of those who spend in the cause of Allah. Each gives in accordance with his or her love of Allah. I do not see that you are able to be of the first or second level, so strive until you go beyond the third level, until you reach some of the lowest grades of the intermediate level.

(continued on page 55)

20   When the word "self" is used on its own, such as "your self" versus "yourself," it is the translation of the word *nafs*. *Nafs* can mean "self," "soul," or "spirit." However, in the context of Sufism, it is usually used to refer to "the evil-commanding self." It is sometimes translated as "ego," but such a translation is not a perfect fit. I have chosen to use "self" instead.

21   Narrated in the hadith collection of al-Tirmidhi (d. 852 CE), a ninth-century scholar of hadith from the city of Tirmidh, in modern-day Uzbekistan. His collection is one of the six relied-upon books of hadith. See also Qur'an 2:271 for more on giving in secret.

22   That is, accepting charity from you.

23   This is also narrated in the hadith collection of al-Tirmidhi. See note 21 above.

Strive so that no time passes except that you give in charity beyond the merely obligatory, even a piece of bread, in order that you raise yourself beyond the level of the miserly. If you do not possess anything to give, then know that charity is not merely given with money, but rather every good word, act of interceding, giving assistance in need, visiting of the sick, following a funeral, all are acts of charity.

Some charity consists of giving something that you are capable of giving, whether it be of your prestige, your self,[20] or your speech, in order that you bring happiness to another's heart.

Guard five matters in your [paying] the poor tax, [offering the] prayer, and [giving] voluntary charity:

1. The first matter is secrecy. The Prophet said, "Charity in secret extinguishes the anger of your Lord."[21] Giving in secret also saves you from showing off, for showing off dominates the self and is destructive.

2. The second matter is that you be on guard against reminding the needy of your charity to them. Its reality is that you see yourself as having done a good deed for the poor person, that you have bestowed a favor on that person. Its sign is that you expect to be thanked or that you dislike if they fall short in fulfilling your rights. Its cure is to know that they are the ones who have been good to you, by accepting from you the right that Allah has over you,[22] as one of the spiritual secrets of the poor tax is the purification of the heart and cleansing it of miserliness and avarice.

3. The third matter is that you give charity from the purest and best of your wealth, for Allah has said, "For they give to Allah that which they dislike" [16:62]. The Prophet said, "Allah does not accept anything except the pure."[23] For the purpose of giving is to express one's love, and the person gives to his or her most beloved the best of what he or she has, not the worst.

(continued on page 57)

24   Dirham is a unit of currency in many Arab countries; however, in al-Ghazali's time, it referred to a specific unit of currency equaling 3.207 ounces of silver. This hadith has been narrated in the collection of al-Nasa'i (d. 915 CE). Al-Nasa'i was a scholar of hadith from Nasa' in modern-day Turkmenistan. His collection is one of the six canonical collections of hadith.

4. The fourth is to give charity with a cheerful face, rejoicing in it, not finding it burdensome. The Prophet said, "One dirham can outstrip a hundred."[24] What is meant by this is that something that you give contentedly and wholeheartedly from the best of your wealth is better than to give a hundred thousand while considering it a burden to do so.

5. The fifth is that you choose for your charity a place whereby its benefits will be multiplied, such as giving your charity to a pious scholar who will use it to piously obey Allah Most High. Alternatively, you might give charity to a righteous relative who has family for whom to provide. Being mindful of virtue is the basis of all matters, for this world is merely a means for Allah's worshippers and a provision for leading them to the hereafter. So you should spend your wealth on those who are traveling to Allah and who have taken this abode as a station in the stages of their journey.

25   Fasting (al-sawm) at minimum consists of abstaining from food, drink, and sexual intercourse from just before dawn until the sun has fully disappeared behind the horizon. There are obligatory and recommended fasts. During the Islamic lunar month of Ramadan, every sane adult Muslim who is not ill, incapacitated, or on a journey is required to fast. There are additional recommended fasts, and you can choose to fast for extra rewards on most any day (with a few exceptions) that you choose.

26   This hadith has been narrated by al-Bukhari and Muslim in their respective collections. Al-Bukhari (d. 870 CE) was born in modern-day Uzbekistan and is considered by many to have gathered the soundest collection of hadith. His collection is therefore the foremost of the six canonical collections. Muslim ibn Hajjaj (d. 875 CE) collected what is considered by many to be the second most authoritative collection of hadiths; however, some scholars consider his collection to be the soundest. He was born in Nishapur, in modern-day Iran, and is said to have been the student of al-Bukhari.

THE THIRD FOUNDATION

☐ Fasting[25]

The Prophet reported that Allah says, "Every good deed is rewarded tenfold up to seven hundred times, except for fasting; fasting is for me, and it is I who reward it."[26] Fasting has this distinction because of two matters:

1. The first is that it relates to restraining the self, which is a hidden matter that is not shown to anyone, unlike prayer, the poor tax, and other works.

2. The second is that it is a subjugation of the enemy of Allah, as the devil is the enemy who only gains strength over you through worldly desires. Hunger breaks all the desires, which are the instruments of the devil.

Know that fasting with respect to both its amount and secrets has three degrees.

As for the degrees of its amount, its least is to fast Ramadan, and its highest is the fast of the Prophet David, who used to alternate, fasting one day and eating throughout the next. It has come in a rigorously authenticated tradition that this is better than fasting every day, for fasting daily would become habitual; the soul is only affected by those things that change its habits, not by the things to which it becomes accustomed. This is similar to medicine; know that the medicine of hearts is close to the medicine of bodies.

(continued on page 61)

27   The Prophet Muhammad recommended fasting on Mondays and Thursdays.

28   That is, engaging in eating, drinking, or sexual intercourse.

29   The voluntary late-night prayers (*tahajjud*) are prayed at the time when most people, except the most devoted, are asleep.

The intermediate level is to fast a third of your days, for if you fast Ramadan and add to it the fasting of Mondays and Thursdays, you have fasted the equivalent of four months.[27] It is not desirable that you fast less than this, for it is light on the self, yet its reward is abundant.

So for the degrees of its spiritual secrets, the lowest is that you simply refrain from the things that nullify the fasts.[28] This is the fasting of commoners, and that is what they are content with when it comes to this term [fasting]. The second is that you add to this the refraining of your limbs from sin, so you guard your tongue from backbiting, your eyes from looking at the prohibited, and likewise all other limbs. The third is that you add to this the guarding of your heart from thoughts and misgivings, and you limit its concerns to the remembrance of Allah. This is the fasting of the most elect and it is the perfection of fasting. Fasting has a completion by which it is perfected; it is that you break your fast on lawful food rather than one of dubious lawfulness. It is also that you not eat excessively such that you compensate completely for what you missed during the day and end up having two meals at once. This causes your stomach to become heavy, your desires to be strengthened, and the spiritual secret of the fast and its benefit is thereby nullified, leading to your being lazy regarding night worship[29] and possibly preventing you from getting up before the dawn prayer.

30   The Hajj is a once-in-a-lifetime pilgrimage to the city of Mecca in modern-day Saudi Arabia that every Muslim who is able must undertake. It consists of not merely a visit to the sacred city, but also a number of rites commemorating the experiences of the Prophet Abraham and his family, as well other more subtle matters.

31   In the first hadith (the Gabriel Hadith) found in the collection of Muslim ibn Hajjaj, for example. See page 58, note 26.

THE FOURTH FOUNDATION

☐ Hajj, the Pilgrimage to Mecca[30]

Allah Most High says in the Qur'an, "Pilgrimage thereto is a duty men owe to Allah, those who can afford the journey; but if any deny faith, Allah stands not in need of any of His creatures" [3:97].

The Prophet mentioned that the Hajj was one of the five pillars of Islam.[31]

The Hajj has outward actions that were mentioned in *The Revival of the Religious Sciences*. What follows is a reminder of some subtle manners and inward spiritual secrets related to the Hajj.

The proper manners are seven:

1. The first is that you choose for the journey a righteous companion and lawful monetary provisions, for lawful money illuminates the heart and a righteous companion reminds you of the good and prevents you from the wrong.

2. The second is that you withhold from engaging in trade, lest your thoughts become distracted and your purpose for the journey not be entirely pure.

3. The third is that you be generous throughout your journey, sharing your food with your companions, and also that you be pleasant in your speech with them.

(continued on page 65)

32　In other words, you should not use excessive or showy means of transportation.

33　This hadith has been related in the collection of Abu Dawud (d. 888–89 CE). Abu Dawud was a Persian scholar of hadith whose collection of hadith is one of the six canonical books of hadith.

34　Mount Arafat is one of the destinations you must visit while on the Hajj. On the second day of the Hajj, pilgrims are required to visit Arafat, the site where the Prophet Muhammad delivered his last sermon. It is a time and place for much supplication, with the expectation that prayers will be answered and sins forgiven.

4. The fourth is that you keep away from vile talk, disputation, and excessive worldly conversation. Rather, you should limit your tongue—beyond mentioning important needs—to the remembrance of Allah and the recitation of the Qur'an.

5. The fifth is that you ride directly on the camel.[32] You should be simple in appearance, without adornment, appearing instead as those in need, so that you are not recorded among those who put on airs.

6. The sixth is that you get off your mount on occasion in order to make it easy for the animal and also to lighten your limbs through some movement. You should not burden your mount with more than it can bear; rather you should be gentle with it.

7. The seventh is that you be content with all that you have had to spend and with whatever has befallen you of tiredness and loss. You should see these as signs of acceptance of your Hajj in order that you anticipate its reward.

As for the secrets of Hajj, these are many, and we will allude to two aspects of them:

1. The first is that the Hajj has been legislated instead of the monasticism that was present in the past religious traditions as has come in the prophetic narrations.[33] Allah has made the Hajj the monastic devotion of the community of Muhammad as He honored the house and ascribed it to Himself and made it the direction of prayer and placed a sacred precinct around it in order to magnify its importance. He made Arafat[34] like the plains at the end of His precincts, and He emphasized its sanctity by prohibiting hunting and cutting of its trees.

(continued on page 67)

35   The various actions of the pilgrimage commemorate something of sacred history, namely, the experiences of Abraham and his family in Mecca. However, there is more to the ritual than commemoration; al-Ghazali explains that your state should be similar to approaching a king's court, but, in this case, the King is the Lord of the Universes (*Rubb al-'Alamin*) and the King of the Day of Judgment (*Malik Yam al-Din*). Although running between two small hills, walking around a building, and other rites of the pilgrimage may seem strange—especially for many in the modern world—these acts are commanded so that they are done out of pure submission to Allah, and not some other motivation.

36   For example, when you leave your family, you should call to mind that you will one day leave them at death. When you leave your homeland, you should call to mind that you will one day leave this world and travel to the next life. When you fear highway bandits along the path, you should remember that you will meet the two questioning angels in the grave (named Munkar and Nakir). For each action, there is a secret wisdom that you may find, so al-Ghazali advises the pilgrim not to merely perform each action of travel as a mere physical motion, but rather to reflect deeply on the inner meaning of each.

He made it like the court of kings in order that visitors direct themselves to it from every place, needy and lowly, humbling themselves before the Lord of the worlds, in submission to His majesty, lowering themselves to His tremendousness, while affirming their absolute transcendence without being bound by a house or contained by a place in order for that to be more emphatic in their expression of slavehood and worshipfulness. This is why Allah made believers responsible for strange acts that do not accord to their temperament or intellect in order that they come to be on the basis of absolute slavehood alone and in fulfillment of the divine command without assistance of any other impulse. This is a tremendous secret of slavehood.[35]

2. This sacred journey has been made like the journey of the hereafter, so the spiritual seeker should remind himself, with each of its actions, of one of the matters of the afterlife that is similar to it, for in each action of the Hajj there is a point of contemplation for the one who contemplates....[36]

37   This hadith was related by Abu Na'im (an eleventh-century Persian scholar of hadith) from al-Nu'man ibn Bashir, a companion of the Prophet Muhammad. In the language of the hadith scholars, it was narrated with a weak chain of transmission. A hadith whose narration from the Prophet has not reached a level of reasonable surety that it was stated by the Prophet is called a "weak hadith." According to many Muslim legal scholars, you may base an action on a weak hadith, under specific conditions, if the action relates to good character or deeds, and not to declaring something permissible or impermissible.

38   This hadith has been narrated in the collection of al-Tirmidhi. See page 54, note 21. In the language of the scholars of hadith, it was narrated with a sound chain of transmission. A sound chain of transmission implies that there is a sufficient degree of surety that the hadith was narrated by the Prophet Muhammad.

39   The *qiblah* is the direction that you face while offering the ritual prayer. The *qiblah* for Muslims is the house of worship in Mecca called the *Ka'ba*. In the early days of Islam, the *qiblah* was Jerusalem. Later in the Prophet's life, the *qiblah* was changed to the *Ka'ba* in Mecca. Both *qiblah*s honored the Abrahamic roots common to Jews, Christians, and Muslims. A *qiblah* unites worshippers in a single direction and purpose; however, Allah is not in any direction, and therefore the Qur'an states: "To Allah belong the East and the West: Whithersoever ye turn, there is the presence of Allah. For Allah is all-Pervading, all-Knowing" [2:115].

THE FIFTH FOUNDATION

☐ Recitation of Qur'an

The Prophet is reported to have said, "The best worship of my community is recitation of the Qur'an."[37]

The Prophet reported that Allah Most High says, "Whomever the Qur'an busies away from calling upon Me and asking of Me, I shall grant him the best of the reward of the thankful."[38]

Know that there are outward and inner manners of reciting the Qur'an.

As for the outward manners, they are three:

1. That you recite it with reverence and veneration. You will not find reverence in your heart until you keep yourself to the outward appearance ... which is to sit calmly in a state of ritual purity with one's head lowered, facing the *qiblah*,[39] without leaning or crossing your legs, nor drowsy. That you recite the Qur'an in a measured way, word by word, without hastiness....

2. That you long to recite it in the times and circumstances when it is most virtuous, that is, that you strive to make your recitation while in the mosque standing in prayer and at night, because the heart is more serene at night, since it is more empty of concerns....

(*continued on page 71*)

40 This has been narrated by al-Tirmidhi and other collectors of hadith with an authentic chain of narration, that is, with a high degree of surety that the Prophet stated it.

41 The throne ('arsh) and the footstool (kursi) are two very large created objects that are manifestations of Allah's power. The size of the rest of the universe in comparison with the footstool is like a person's ring in the desert. The size of the footstool in relation to the throne is also like a ring in comparison to the size of the desert. Allah is not confined by time and space and is in no need of a location in which to reside, so these objects have been created to manifest Allah's sovereignty and might. Just as a throne for humans is elevated and made grandiose to humble those around it, Allah's throne and footstool are also elevated, at the farthest point of the universe. The throne is the largest of all created objects and has been called the ceiling or roof of creation. There are many references to the throne and footstool in the Qur'an, including ayat al-kursi (2:255).

However you recite it, even if leaning and without purification, it is not bereft of virtue, for Allah Most High has extolled all who recite it, saying, "Those who celebrate the praises of Allah, standing, sitting, and lying down on their sides, and contemplate the (wonders of) creation in the heavens and the earth, (with the thought): 'Our Lord! not for naught hast Thou created (all) this! Glory to Thee! Give us salvation from the penalty of the Fire'" [3:191]....

If you are of those who seek the hereafter, leaving virtue is not easy for you.

3. The amount of recitation, and it has three levels. The lowest is that you complete it once a month. The most is that you repeat it every three days. The Prophet said, "Whoever recites the Qur'an in less than three days will not have understood it."**40** The medium extent is that you complete it once a week....

As for its inward proper manners, these are five:

1. That you feel from the beginning of your recitation the tremendousness of the words by feeling the tremendousness of the Speaker [i.e., Allah]. You should bring to your heart and mind the throne and footstool,**41** and the heavens and earth, and all they contain of the angels, jinn, humans, animals, and minerals; remind yourself that the Creator of all of them is One. Also (bring to mind) that everything is in the grasp of His power, between His grace and mercy. Also (call to mind) that you are seeking to recite His speech, to behold through it His attributes, and to discern the beauty of His knowledge and wisdom....

(continued on page 73)

42   Ali was the Prophet Muhammad's son-in-law and cousin. He was one of the earliest converts to Islam and later became the caliph, or ruler, of the Muslims after the death of the Prophet. The Shia sect of Islam considers Ali to have been the rightful heir to spiritual and political leadership after the death of the Prophet.

You know that just as the outward text of the Qur'an can only be touched by those in a state of outward ritual purity, and others are also prevented from touching it, likewise the reality of its meanings and inward aspect is veiled from the innermost of the heart, except from one who has purified himself of all inward vileness and filth....

2. That you recite it while reflecting on its meanings.... And everything your tongue recites in a state of heedlessness, repeat it. Ali[42] said, "There is no virtue in worship without understanding, nor in recitation without reflection...."

3. That you seek from your reflection the fruits of understanding from their boughs.... That which is mentioned in the Qur'an that relates to Allah Most High, His attributes, and His actions, understand from it Allah's majesty and grandeur. That which relates to guidance to the straight path, take from it understanding of Allah's mercy, gentleness, and wisdom. That which relates to the destruction of Allah's enemies, take from it understanding of Allah's might and honor, His being free of need, and His overwhelming power. That which relates to the prophets, take from it understanding of divine gentleness and blessings and favor and generosity, and so on....

4. That you rid yourself of things that prevent you from understanding.... As for believers who direct themselves to the path to Allah mighty and majestic, they are veiled by two types of things (that prevent them from understanding):

   a. Whisperings that distract the heart by thinking about intention, and whether you had it, or whether you are sincere right now. These occur in the ritual prayer.

(continued on page 75)

43   "Gaining light" might best be explained as gaining spiritual illumination. It refers to an experience gained from sincere worship. One who
is very pious is often described as having a face full of *nur*. An English
equivalent might be found in the expression "her face was beaming."
Al-Ghazali is recommending that you go beyond this illumined state,
toward higher spiritual states that bring you closer to the goal of
experiential knowledge of Allah.

Additionally, there are misgivings that cause you to worry excessively about proper pronunciation of the letters and thereby repeating your recitation on account of that. This happens in the ritual prayer and at other times. So, how can a heart behold the spiritual secrets of the higher worlds if the heart is veiled by its consideration of how your lips are moving and the sounds that they are producing?

b.   Rigid adherence to the mere outward meanings of the Qur'an and remaining with those. This is a tremendous veil from understanding. I do not mean merely the following of false understanding, such as following a heretical innovator, but rather even following a sound understanding. For the truth that people have been made responsible to believe has degrees that have an outward beginning that is like the outward shell, and it has an inward depth that is its essence.... Those who hold themselves to the outward, thinking that there is no meaning beyond it toward which they should ascend, how can spiritual secrets be unveiled for them?

5.   That you not limit yourself to gaining light,[43] but that you add to it the gaining of spiritual states and traces. That is achieved by not reciting any verse except that you characterize yourself by its traits so that you experience a state in accordance with each verse that you recite. So, when mercy and forgiveness are mentioned, you should rejoice as if you are flying out of joy. When anger and intensity of punishment is mentioned, you diminish as if you are dying out of fear. When Allah and His names and might are mentioned, you lower yourself and become diminished as if you are being completely extinguished in beholding the divine majesty. When those who deny faith mention that which is absurd for Allah of child and companion, you become shy and lower your voice as if you will melt away out of shyness, and so on....

(continued on page 77)

44 That is, into your physical (*mulk*) and spiritual (*malakut*) dimensions, as well as the dimension of witnessing the Divine (*jabarut*).

Let the traces of this appear on your limbs, through crying when saddened, a sweating forehead when shy, and quivering of your skin out of awe and majesty. Let your limbs and tongue expand when gladdened, and contract when in awe. If you do this, then each of your limbs will have shared of something of the Qur'an, and the effects of the Qur'an will overflow into all three of your worlds.... **44**

Know that the Qur'an is like the sun, and the overflowing from it [the Qur'an] of the spiritual secrets of knowledge into the heart are like the overflowing of the light of the sun upon the earth. The flowing of the traces of fear, reverence, awe, and all other states on the heart are like the flowing of the heat of the sun in the earth after the dawning of its light, for awe of the Divine is the trace of the light of knowing Allah. Allah Most High says, "Those truly fear Allah, among His Servants, who have knowledge, for Allah is exalted in might, oft-forgiving" [35:28]....

45   Remembrance of Allah (see the Introduction, page xxviii), or *dhikr*, is the central aspect of Islamic ritual. It is contrasted with forgetting Allah, which is one of the roots of sin. Remembering Allah is the goal of all acts of worship and obedience, because without it, worship and action would be merely movements and speech. There are many forms of *dhikr*, including the recitation of supplications, litanies, or the names of Allah. Some forms of *dhikr* are done through spoken recitation; others are done silently and solely in the heart.

46   Related in the hadith collections of al-Tirmidhi and Ibn Majah (d. 887 CE). Ibn Majah was a Persian hadith scholar from the city of Qazwin in modern-day Iran. His collection of hadith is one of the six canonical collections of hadith.

47   This implies that recitation of the Qur'an, repetition of litanies, or chanting the names of Allah is done by rote, without contemplating or comprehending the meanings of the words. The supplicant who realizes he or she is reciting by rote and considers quitting as a result is often advised to persist because the heart and tongue are like upstairs and downstairs neighbors; if the upstairs neighbor makes enough noise, the downstairs neighbor may eventually want to know what all the racket is about.

THE SIXTH FOUNDATION

☐ Regarding Remembrance of Allah Mighty and Majestic in Every State⁴⁵

Allah Most High says in the Qur'an, "And when the prayer is finished, then may ye disperse through the land, and seek of the Bounty of Allah, and celebrate the praises of Allah often (and without stint), that ye may prosper" [62:10].

He Most High also said to His Prophet, "But keep in remembrance the name of thy Lord and devote thyself to Him wholeheartedly" [73:8].

The Prophet said, "Shall I not inform you of the best of your actions, and the purest with your Master, those that raise you to the highest ranks, and are better for you than giving gold and silver, better for you than meeting your enemies and striking their necks and their striking yours?" And they responded, "What is that, O messenger of Allah?" He said, "Remembrance of Allah."⁴⁶

Know that it has been disclosed to the people of spiritual insight that remembrance of Allah is the best of your deeds. However, it also has three outer layers as well as an essential core that is beneath them. The merit of these outer layers is their being a path to the core:

1. The outermost layer is the remembrance with the tongue alone.⁴⁷

(continued on page 81)

48   Such a heart remembers Allah when you watch over it, supervising the heart and making an effort to keep it focused. This second layer pertains to a person who has gone beyond merely reciting litanies or chanting the names of Allah, to struggling to remain mentally present while contemplating the meanings of words recited. At this point, you are not fully present with your litanies, nor fully absent, but rather, you oscillate between the two states.

49   The valley of thoughts (*fikr*; pl. *afkar*) is contrasted with remembrance (*dhikr*; pl. *adhkar*). *Fikr* gives the impression of the mind's contemplation as an intellectual process, whereas *dhikr* gives the impression of the heart's recollection as a spiritual process. When the heart is not involved in the remembrance of Allah, it may follow the mind to wherever it may wander.

50   This layer, being the closest to the essential core of the remembrance of Allah, refers to a person who is deeply immersed in remembrance of Allah and is only distracted from this state through some extraordinary effort or circumstances.

51   That is, the supplicant becomes unaware of the spiritual practice of *dhikr* and the heart's focus, and instead becomes immersed in the state of annihilation, discussed below.

52   Not included in this translation is al-Ghazali's extensive discussion of the concept of annihilation (*fana'*), due in part to its length but also its complexity. The state of *fana'* is so rare that attempts to explain it and other high states of Sufism tend to fall short for the reader who has not experienced them. That said, in the technical terminology of the Sufis, *fana'* refers to the state wherein everything in the universe, from your own body and inner thoughts to your physical surroundings, disappears from your perception, and all that remains is your spiritual perception of Allah.

53   This hadith has been narrated in the hadith collection of al-Tabarani (d. 970–71), a well-known scholar of hadith from Syria. Al-Tirmidhi has narrated a more popularly known hadith of greater authenticity with a similar meaning.

2. The second layer is the remembrance with the heart, when such a heart requires supervision in order that it becomes present with the remembrance.[48] If such a heart leaves the remembrance of Allah, and that becomes his disposition, then it is left to wander in the valleys of thoughts.[49]

3. The third layer is that the remembrance takes possession of the heart and becomes firmly established in it, such that great effort is required to turn it away from remembrance toward something else, much like the need of the heart discussed in the second layer above required great effort to establish the presence of the remembrance with it and persevere in it.[50]

4. The forth layer is the essential core itself. It is that that which is remembered becomes firmly established in the heart, while the remembrance itself vanishes and disappears.[51] This is the essential core that is sought. This is the state that those who know of Allah experientially call annihilation.[52]

This is the beneficial fruit of the essential core of remembrance of Allah. It begins with the remembrance of the tongue, then the remembrance of the heart with great effort, then the remembrance of the heart by natural disposition, then that which is remembered overtakes the heart and the remembrance itself vanishes. This is the secret of the Prophet's saying, "Whoever desires to graze in the gardens of paradise, increase in the remembrance of Allah mighty and majestic."[53]

(*continued on page 83*)

54   This is the state described as the essential core of remembrance, wherein the heart is overcome by its witnessing of Allah, and the act of remembrance disappears.

55   In this state there is no multiplicity; you do not perceive the individual parts of the created universe, but rather only experience the unity of its Creator.

56   There are a number of hadiths narrated in the collections of Ibn Majah, al-Tirmidhi, al-Tabarani, and others that mention which chapters or verses of the Qur'an possess Allah's greatest name.

57   Al-Ghazali's definition helps distinguish between biological life in particular, and life in its more general meaning of that which is sentient or self-aware.

58   In other words, "the Eternal" (*al-Qayyum*), being one of Allah's divine names, points to His divine attribute of self-subsistence, meaning that Allah is not dependent on anything else.

59   "Glorified is Allah" (*subhan Allah*) indicates Allah's glory and sanctity in such a way that can only be ascribed to Him. It is a phrase that Muslims might say when in a state of awe.

60   "All praise is due to Allah" (*al-hamdu illah*) expresses your appreciation that all blessings, physical or otherwise, are from Allah.

61   "There is no God but Allah" (*la ilaha illa Allah*) is an expression of recognition of Allah's sole right to being worshipped, because He is singular in His divinity and Godhood. It is also an expression of your recognition of His unity in His being (there being no partitions or multiple beings making up His entity), in His attributes (there being no co-sharer in His will, power, knowledge, and so on), and in His actions (there being no other being with actual power to create or cause a particular effect).

62   "Allah is Greatest" (*Allahu Akbar*) does not mean that Allah is the greatest out of a set of other things, for there is no other like Allah. All created things, al-Ghazali says, are lights from the light of His power. In other words, created things are the traces or effects of His power. Rather, with "Allah is Greatest," al-Ghazali is saying that Allah is greater than can be grasped by the senses, perceived by the intellect, or known comprehensively in His full reality.

If one were to ask which is the most meritorious expression of remembrance, know that the best, discussed above, is the overwhelming of the heart by that which is remembered.[54] This is the essence of Islamic monotheism.....[55]

Among the best expressions of remembrance is "There is no God but Allah, the Living, the Eternal." Within this phrase there is Allah's greatest name.[56] The meaning of "Living" is that He is self-aware, and the meaning of "dead" is that one has no awareness of oneself.[57] "The Eternal" informs one that He is self-subsistent and that all others subsist through Him.[58]

[Also among the best expressions of remembrance is] your saying, "Glorified is Allah,[59] all praise is due to Allah,[60] there is no God but Allah,[61] and Allah is Greatest....."[62]

This suffices, for now, as a hint as to the secrets of remembrance and its most meritorious forms.

63   In other words, there is a connection between what you eat and the quality and acceptability of your acts of worship.

64   This hadith has been reported in the collections of al-Tabarani and al Bayhaqi (d. 1066), the latter scholar being an important Persian scholar of law and hadith. Al-Ghazali explains the meaning of "primary obligations" as indicating belief and the ritual prayer (*salah*). In other words, after accepting the message of the Qur'an and establishing the daily ritual prayer in one's life, one of the most central obligations in a person's life is to seek pure and lawful food.

65   "Both" refers to Abdullah and his father, Umar, the latter being one of the Prophet's primary companions, and also the second caliph (ruler) after the Prophet's death. It is common among Muslims to refer to people by their first name and then the name of their father, the word *ibn* meaning "son," and *bint* meaning "daughter." So, "Abdullah ibn Umar" means "Abdullah, the son of Umar."

THE SEVENTH FOUNDATION

☐ Seeking the Permissible

Allah Most High says in the Qur'an, "O ye apostles! enjoy (all) things good and pure, and work righteousness, for I am well-acquainted with (all) that ye do" [23:51].

That which is forbidden is bad and evil, not pure and good. Allah Most High linked pure and good food with worship.[63]

The Prophet said, "Seeking the permissible is obligatory for every Muslim, after the primary obligations."[64]

Abdullah ibn Umar[65] said, "Acts of worship that have been accompanied by forbidden food are like building on manure."

(continued on page 87)

66   Spiritual practice and its effectiveness are directly connected to the kind of food you eat—permissible or forbidden. According to al-Ghazali, there is within the subject of seeking lawful food a spiritual secret that is so weighty, it could not be mentioned in this book. Perhaps what is intended here is that some things can only be experienced; in this case, the spiritual secret experienced from being scrupulous in what you eat may only be known to those who achieve that level of scrupulousness. In any case, the translator is not privy to this secret.

67   This refers to a person's suitability to be a certain type of witness in a court case. Islam is careful about whose testimony is acceptable in specific cases, and a person who openly and knowingly eats forbidden food is considered of questionable integrity and therefore not a valid witness. This illustrates the significance of Islam's dietary restrictions, in that a person who eats improperly slaughtered chicken, for example, would not have his or her testimony accepted in specific court cases.

68   There are matters of consensus in Islam and matters of valid scholarly disagreement. For example, some scholars consider eating shrimp to be permissible, based on interpretation of certain evidence, while others consider it impermissible based on differing interpretations. A person who is at this second level of cautiousness might abandon eating shrimp if he or she did not have certainty in its permissibility or impermissibility.

69   This hadith has been rigorously authenticated and narrated in the collections of Ahmad, al-Nasa'i, Ibn Hibban (d. 965 CE), and al-Tirmidhi. Ibn Hibban was born in modern-day Afghanistan, of Arab descent, and is the author of an important collection of hadith, as well as numerous other works.

Lawful Food and the Purification of the Heart

Know that lawful food has an important property with regard to the purification and illumination of the heart and in assuring its acceptance of the lights of spiritual knowledge. Within this subject, there is a secret whose mention this book could not carry.[66] It is necessary that you understand there are four degrees of scrupulousness with regard to your food:

1. The first is the scrupulousness of the upright. It is that those who eat from impermissible food are rendered grave sinners, and their probity is revoked[67] when they abandon this level of cautiousness. It is that you avoid that which the legal scholars of law have declared forbidden.

2. The second is the scrupulousness of the pious. It is that you are on guard against that which borders on impermissible, even if a legal scholar declares it permissible.[68] This is what the Prophet referred to when he said, "Leave what gives you doubt for that which does not give you doubt."[69]

(continued on page 89)

70   Meaning "servant of Allah." It also carries the meaning of "worshipper."

71   An example is given in al-Ghazali's *The Revival of the Religious Sciences* of a man who went to visit a dying friend at nighttime. When the friend passed away, the man put out the lamp, in recognition that the lamp oil now belonged to the deceased's inheritors.

72   In other words, a person at this level avoids neutral actions that do not lead to meritorious actions as well as those actions that may not be impermissible in and of themselves, but are potential inroads to sin, albeit a step or two removed from the bad action itself.

73   Dhul Nun al-Misri (d. 859 CE) was one of the early Sufis. He was very pious and lived an ascetic life. He is often cited as an example of extreme piety by many Muslims, whether they identify themselves with Sufism or not.

74   The food itself was permissible, purchased from the woman's wealth, which was earned through permissible means, yet since it passed through the hands of an oppressor, he avoided the food because of its proximity to sin, not because it was sinful in and of itself.

75   The prohibitions and commandments of Islam are not merely a checklist of do's and don'ts, but rather they are a means to spiritual enlightenment through drawing nearer to Allah. Nor is the purpose of following the laws of Islam merely to avoid hell and enjoy the physical pleasures of paradise, but it is also to lead to a spiritual reward in this life through spiritual illumination and, ultimately, experiential knowledge of Allah (*ma'rifah*).

76   Here, al-Ghazali quotes a part of a hadith found in the collections of al-Bukhari and Muslim ibn Hajjaj. In questionable cases, you give others the benefit of the doubt and consider their wealth and what comes from it permissible. The idea is to strike a balance between cautiousness and suspicion, thus warding off extremes that lead to prohibiting the permissible.

3. The third is the scrupulousness of the God-fearing. The Prophet said, "The servant[70] does not reach the level of the God-fearing until he leaves that in which there is no objection out of cautiousness and fear of that which is objectionable. Umar is reported to have said, 'We have given up nine-tenths of the permissible for fear of the unlawful....'"[71]

4. The fourth is the scrupulousness of the truthful. It is that you are wary of everything that is not undertaken with the intention of obtaining the power to obey Allah or that you are wary of that which leads to the causes of disobedience.[72] An example of this is what has been related regarding Dhul Nun al-Misri[73] while he was (wrongfully) imprisoned and hungry. A pious woman sent him some food, via the prison warden, from her pure and permissible wealth. Al-Misri refused to eat it, as it had been delivered at the hands of the oppressor....[74]

Know that which you are on guard against from the impermissible is the darkening of the heart, while that which is sought from the permissible is the heart's illumination.[75]

Worldly Wealth Is Not Entirely Forbidden

You might be excessively harsh with yourself and declare that all the wealth of the world is forbidden, but rather, know decisively that "the permissible is clear, and the forbidden is clear, and between the two are uncertain matters."[76]

77   Much of what is mentioned in this section applies not just to your coreligionists but also to all humanity.

78   Muslims believe that all people are on the journey of life, which began in pre-eternity when all were raised before Allah and asked, "Am I not your Lord?" All responded "Yes!" What followed was life in the womb and then this worldly life, which is a test that determines your suitability for Allah's mercy and reward or His justice and punishment. After this worldly life comes the life of the grave, which will be like a valley of paradise for some and a pit of hell for others. Then comes the resurrection, and all the trials and experiences associated with it, followed by eternal reward in paradise for some, eternal punishment in hell for others, and temporary punishment followed by eternal reward for still others. This is the journey of the human soul. How you are with your fellow travelers is a crucial aspect of the spiritual path.

79   Al-Ghazali calls these different beings "armies," with the meaning of "servants," as in the following passage.

80   *The Marvels of the Heart* can be found in translation on www.Ghazali.org or in print as *The Marvels of the Heart: Science of the Spirit* (Louisville, KY: Fons Vitae, 2010).

81   In *The Marvels of the Heart*, al-Ghazali mentions that anger and desire can serve and assist the intellect and the rest of the internal armies. He describes the limbs in *The Marvels of the Heart* as being the external armies or servants of the heart, and various inner inclinations as being the internal armies or servants of the heart. He gives an example of the intellect functioning as the king who rules over the city of the body. Desire and anger are portrayed as being enemies who seek to destroy the citizens of the city, whom the king must protect by overcoming the enemy. The body is like the frontier outposts, and the soul the guardhouse. If they succeed in overcoming the enemy, then your actions will be righteous and praised on the Day of Judgment.

THE EIGHTH FOUNDATION

☐ Establishing the Rights of the Believers⁷⁷ and Keeping Good Company

Establishing the rights of the believers and keeping good company with them is one of the pillars of the religion, since the meaning of "the religion" is the journey to Allah Most High. Among the pillars of the journey is keeping good company with your fellow travelers in the way stations of the journey, and all people are journeying....**78**

Know that you are with regard to the world either by yourself, with your family, children, relatives, and neighbors, or with the general masses. For each of these three states, you must be good company and render the rights of others.

1.   The first state is that you are by yourself. Know that within yourself is a universe and that its interior comprises various kinds of beings,**79** differing in their nature and manners. If you do not keep good company with them and render their rights unto them, then you perish. There are many types of internal armies, as mentioned in the Qur'anic verse "... None can know the forces [armies] of thy Lord, except He, and this is no other than a warning to mankind" [74:31].

A careful examination of these may be found in the book *The Marvels of the Heart*, which is in *The Revival of the Religious Sciences*.**80**

Mentioned here are a few of the most important armies. You have within you desires by which you attract to yourself benefits, anger by which you repel from yourself harm, and an intellect by which you contemplate various issues....**81**

(continued on page 93)

82   In another example from *The Marvels of the Heart*, al-Ghazali likens anger to a hunting dog, and desire to a horse. A skilled horseman with a tamed horse and a trained dog will likely succeed in the hunt. He likens a clumsy horseman to an ignorant man who does not use his intellect properly, an unruly horse to the victory of desire over the soul—especially in matters related to excesses in food and sexual appetites—and the vicious dog to the domination of anger. When you can overcome anger, experiencing the emotion only when it is justified—such as over your bad actions or injustice in the world—then the hunter's dog is well trained and able to assist in the hunt. When you overcome your desires and only desire that which is good, then your horse will carry you safely to your goal.

83   At bare minimum, you should seek to avoid offending people, speaking ill of them, or in any other way causing emotional, physical, financial, or spiritual harm. There are many Qur'anic exhortations and prophetic sayings to this effect, including the advice to be silent except in saying what is good, never to even say "uff" to your parents, and that even removing something harmful from the road is a branch of faith.

84   This hadith can be found in the collections of al-Bukhari and Muslim ibn Hajjaj.

85   The word *'iyal* (dependents) is usually used in the sense of close family whom you support. While Allah is transcendently beyond likeness to His creation, including having family, the intent of "dependents" here is that all of creation is dependent on Allah and that there is a sense of concern and care for them.

86   This hadith can be found in the collection of al-Tabarani and other hadith collections.

87   This hadith has been narrated by Ibn Mardawayh (d. 1019–20)—a Persian narrator of hadiths who is not as well known to nonspecialists as many of the other hadith narrators mentioned thus far—and in similar form by al-Bayhaqi.

You are, with regard to your anger, a dog, and with regard to your desires, a beast of burden, such as a horse. With regard to your intellect, you are a king. You are commanded to be fair between each of them, to render unto them their rights, and to seek their help, so that you might attain eternal felicity by their aid. If you tame the horse, and train the dog, and subject them to the king, they will take you to the victory that you seek.[82]

2. The second state is your keeping company of the general masses. The lowest degree of being good company is that you refrain from harming them.[83] The Prophet said, "The Muslim is one from whose tongue and hand the Muslims are safe."[84] Over and above that is that you seek to benefit them and act kindly toward them. The Prophet said, "All people are the dependents[85] of Allah; the most beloved of them to Allah are those who are most beneficial to His dependents."[86] Above and beyond this is that you remove harm from them, and this is the level of the truthful. The Prophet said, "If you want to surpass the Truthful, separate from one who cuts you off, give to one who forbids you, and forgive one who oppresses you."[87] This is the totality of the affair.

(*continued on page 95*)

88 Al-Ghazali lists here twenty examples of good character and manners toward people in general. I have translated and explained a sample from them.

89 As stated in the Qur'an, "Serve Allah, and join not any partners with Him; and do good to parents, kinsfolk, orphans, those in need, neighbors who are near, neighbors who are strangers, the companion by your side, the wayfarer (ye meet), and what your right hands possess. For Allah loveth not the arrogant, the vainglorious" [4:36].

90 Regarding the rights of parents, the Qur'an says, "Thy Lord hath decreed that ye worship none but Him, and that ye be kind to parents …" [17:23–24].

Regarding the rights of children, the Prophet said, "Whoever fails to show mercy to our children or does not acknowledge the right of our elderly is not from among us." This is found in the hadith collection *al-Adab al-Mufrad* by al-Bukhari.

Regarding the rights of your spouse, the Qur'an says, "And among His Signs is this, that He created for you mates from among yourselves, that ye may dwell in tranquility with them, and He has put love and mercy between your (hearts); verily in that are Signs for those who reflect" [30:21].

The Prophet said, "The best of you is the best to your family, and I am the best of you to my family."

91 Prior to Islam, there were no checks and balances on the institution of slavery. With the coming of Islam, severe restrictions were placed on the institution, and many rights given to the individual, with the end goal being emancipation and returning him or her to society. Despite the absence of slavery in the Qur'anic sense in the modern world, the rights mentioned in al-Ghazali's text are worth contemplating, considering that many free people today have fewer rights than a slave in the time of the Prophet. Al-Ghazali sums up the intent of the various hadiths with this: "The upshot of the rights of the servant is that you share with him from your own food and clothing, that you do not overburden him beyond his capacity, that you excuse his lapses, and do not look at him from a position of pride or contempt, and teach him the requirements of his religion."

The explanation of these rights are many, however they can be summarized as follows.[88]

- That you love for the people what you love for yourself.

- That you have a cheerful disposition with all people.

- That you neither listen to nor spread what people say about each other.

- That you are wary of the gatherings of the wealthy, and that you frequent the gatherings of the poor.

- That you avoid keeping the company of any except those who benefit you in your religion or whom you can benefit.

The upshot of all of the above is that you do to others what you would like them to do to you with regard to excellent character, concern, and avoiding harm.

3. The third state is your keeping the company of those with whom you have a specific relationship, such as

- neighbors,[89]

- close kin,[90]

- and servants....[91]

92   This means that you love your friend for the sake of Allah, to the extent that that person becomes like a family member. In the chapter on the duties of brotherhood in *The Revival of the Religious Sciences*, al-Ghazali mentions that such a friendship entails favoring your friends' needs over your own and assisting your friends financially, for example. See Muhtar Holland, *The Duties of Brotherhood in Islam*, new impression ed. (Leicester: Islamic Foundation, 1988).

93   This is what is called a *hadith qudsi*. It is the Prophet using his own words to express something that Allah has said. It is different in this sense from the Qur'an, which is the word of Allah narrated via the angel Gabriel to the Prophet Muhammad. This hadith, narrated in the collection of Malik ibn Anas (d. 795)—founder of the Maliki school of law from Medina—and others, indicates that friendship for the sake of Allah is a means to salvation. "My shade" does not mean that Allah casts a shadow; He is transcendently different from creation, including being limited by time and space. Rather, it means that on a day of great dread and trial, Allah will protect certain people because of their selfless love for others.

94   In the context of Sufism, the term *shaykh* refers to one's spiritual guide (*murshid*), which is how I interpret al-Ghazali's use of the term in this passage. You love your spiritual teachers because through them you learn knowledge, practice, and character that will lead you to success in this life and, most important, in the next.

95   This is the highest form of love, especially if you love another for this reason solely, and not to obtain something, even something meritorious such as knowledge or spiritual assistance. Al-Ghazali goes on to explain that if someone loves another conditioned by some type of spiritual benefit, despite the merit of seeking such a benefit, such a person is weak in faith. For those who would like further explanation, al-Ghazali refers the reader to the chapter on the duties of brotherhood in *The Revival of the Religious Sciences*.

The Duties of Brotherhood

From among the roots of the religion with regard to the command to being good company is taking a brother for the sake of Allah Mighty and Majestic.**92** The Prophet said, "Allah says on the Day of Judgment, 'Where are those who loved each other for my Majesty? Today I will shade them from my shade, on a day when there is no shade except my shade.'"**93**

Know that every love that cannot be conceived of without belief in Allah and the Last Day, that is love for the sake of Allah Most High. However, it is of two degrees:

1. The first is that you love someone in order to obtain a connection in this world, connecting you to the afterlife, such as your love of your teacher or your *shaykh*.**94**

2. The second, and it is the highest rank, is that you love someone because he is beloved by Allah Mighty and Majestic and because he loves Allah.**95**

96 Many hadiths have been transmitted about the obligation to command righteous actions and forbid evil actions. Among them, found in the hadith collection of Muslim ibn Hajjaj, is "Whoever of you sees a wrong action, let him change it with his hand. If he cannot do so, then with his tongue. If unable, then with his heart, and that is the weakest degree of faith."

97 Before summarizing the gist of the topic, al-Ghazali gave several examples of wrongful actions, omitted in the translation, such as those who attend gatherings where people are wearing forbidden clothing, rooms are decorated with prohibited images, people are intentionally leaving out integrals of their prayers, and scholarly sessions of exhortation, debate, or discussion occur wherein harmful and impermissible things are spoken.

THE NINTH FOUNDATION

☐ Commanding the Right and Forbidding the Wrong

Allah Most High says in the Qur'an, "Let there arise out of you a band of people inviting to all that is good, enjoining what is right, and forbidding what is wrong. They are the ones to attain felicity" [3:104].

He Most High also says, "The Believers, men and women, are protectors one of another: they enjoin what is just, and forbid what is evil; they observe regular prayers, practice regular charity, and obey Allah and His Messenger. On them will Allah pour His mercy, for Allah is exalted in power, wise" [9:71].

He Most High also says, "Nor did they (usually) forbid one another the iniquities which they committed; evil indeed were the deeds which they did" [5:79].**96**

Whoever Is Silent in the Presence of a Wrong Action Shares Responsibility for It

All who witness a wrong action and do not forbid it—remaining silent about it—share in its responsibility....

The upshot of all this **97** is that whoever mingles with people, his bad actions increase—even if he is pious and God-fearing in his own actions—unless he leaves hypocrisy and busies himself with commanding the right and forbidding the evil. The obligation to do so only falls from him in two cases:

(continued on page 101)

98 Since being a scholar of law can bring power and influence, it is not uncommon to find some corrupt scholars. They may be masters of the legal texts and the application of legal principles, but they may also openly commit certain sins.

99 Drinking alcohol is strictly forbidden in Islam, owing to its negative effects on society being greater than its potential benefits. Attending a gathering where people are drinking, when there is no requirement to do so (e.g., a meeting at work or family gathering), is also a sin.

100 Al-Ghazali mentions in *The Revival of the Religious Sciences* and elsewhere some additional conditions for commanding righteous actions and forbidding wrongful ones, such as having proper knowledge regarding the issue, avoiding spying on people, and there being no scholarly disagreement over the matter. He also mentions levels of commanding and forbidding, which include informing, followed by politely counseling if informing does not work, then using harsh language, then taking physical action against objects (such as breaking wine bottles), then threatening violence against the person (such as forcibly shutting down an opium den). Since the last could lead to civil strife, this falls under the responsibility of the government. Indeed, some have interpreted the hadith mentioned earlier as changing a wrong with one's hand being the role of government, changing with argument being the role of the scholars, and being displeased in your heart with something sinful being the duty of the common person without authority to act or speak on a matter.

1.   The first is that he knows that if he forbids [a wrong action], his advice will not be heeded, the action will not be left undone, and he will be looked upon with derision and mockery. This is what happens the majority of times with regard to the wrong actions committed by the scholars of law.[98] If a person knows that the one committing the wrong action is a person of religious knowledge, he may remain silent, but it is better to reprimand him verbally, manifesting the badge of religion. It is necessary that he leave the place in which the wrong action occurs, for it is not permissible to witness a bad action by choice. Whoever sits in a gathering in which people are drinking alcohol, he is a grave sinner, even if he does not drink.[99]

2.   The second case is that he knows that he is able to prevent the wrong action, such that if he sees a bottle of wine and is able to break it, but he knows that he will be hit or injured for doing so, then it is still meritorious [but not obligatory] for him to do so, according to the Qur'anic verse "... Establish regular prayer, enjoin what is just, and forbid what is wrong; and bear with patient constancy whatever betide thee; for this is firmness (of purpose) in (the conduct of) affairs" [31:17]. It is not necessary for him to take action though, except when several qualifications are met, mentioned in *The Revival of the Religious Sciences*.

The upshot is that the obligation to command and forbid is not canceled except when coerced in his body by being hit, or in his wealth by it being liquidated, or in his honor and rank through contempt by way of slandering his valor. As for fear of alienation or objection being brought against him, the obligation to command the right and forbid the wrong does not fall from him.[100]

101 A person who is dour and harsh in attempting to correct the actions of others often turns people away and sometimes causes people to associate harshness and negativity with the rules and regulations of religion. However, as mentioned previously, the rules and regulations of religion are meant to draw you nearer to Allah as a form of remembrance throughout the day, disrupting your egotistical inclinations and calling you to higher spiritual realities. The Prophet did not yell, scream, and wag his finger at those who were committing wrong actions. He was gentle in his admonitions and patient with those who were obstinate.

102 Hasan al-Basri was an important early Muslim who lived in Basra in modern-day Iraq. There are many pious statements attributed to him, as well as legal and theological positions.

103 While your do not need to wait to perfect yourself before being a voice for change in your community, hypocrisy should be strictly avoided.

Important Issues Pertaining to Commanding the Right and Forbidding the Wrong

There are two important issues with regard to commanding the right and forbidding the wrong:

1. The first is kindness and gentleness, in that you should begin the admonition with softness, not harshness.[101]

2. The second issue is that the one commanding and forbidding begins with himself first, purifying his self and leaving that which he forbids. Hasan al-Basri[102] said, "If you are one who forbids bad actions, be one of those who follows such admonitions; otherwise, you will be ruined." However, this is not a necessary condition; rather it is permissible for a sinner to command and forbid as well.[103]

104 *Sunnah* literally means "the trodden path," and in this context refers to the demonstrative example of the Prophet Muhammad. The *sunnah* is not synonymous with hadith, which are the recorded sayings, actions, and tacit approvals of the Prophet. The hadith is one of the avenues by which the *sunnah* was recorded. Another avenue, according to some early scholars, was the living example of communities of early Muslims who lived in places where many of the Prophet's companions settled after his death. One such scholar was Malik ibn Anas, after whom the Maliki school of law is named. He believed that the actions of the learned people of the city of Medina in his time (*'amal ahl madinah*) were a means of transmitting the *sunnah* of the Prophet.

105 Al-Ghazali explains, in a passage omitted from the translation, that this entails wearing pants while sitting and a turban while standing; eating with one's right hand; clipping one's fingernails and toenails, starting from the right hand followed by the left, then the right foot followed by the left, and so on. He also narrates a story about a pious man who refused to eat watermelon because he did not know the Prophet's manner in eating one.

THE TENTH FOUNDATION

☐ Regarding Following the *Sunnah*

Know that the key to happiness is following the Prophet's example[104] and imitating the messenger of Allah in all of your points of departure and arrival, movement and stillness, to the extent that you imitate the manners of the Prophet's manner of eating, standing, sleeping, and speech. This does not merely regard following his manners solely in your worship, but rather in all matters....[105]

Allah Most High says in the Qur'an, "Say: 'If ye do love Allah, follow Me; Allah will love you and forgive you your sins. For Allah is oft-Forgiving, most merciful'" [3:31].

He Most High says, "What Allah has bestowed on His Messenger (and taken away) from the people of the townships belongs to Allah, to His Messenger, and to kindred and orphans, the needy and the wayfarer; in order that it may not (merely) make a circuit between the wealthy among you. So take what the Messenger assigns to you, and deny yourselves that which he withholds from you. And fear Allah, for Allah is strict in punishment" [59:7].

One should not be negligent in these regards, saying, "These are matters connected to customary habits, not matters of the *sunnah.*" Saying such would shut upon you one of the great gates to felicity!

106 "Rectification" and "uprightness" are common translations for *ta'dil* and *'adl*, both being derived from the same three root letters *'a-d-l*. Both words also have the implied meaning of straightness, as opposed to crookedness. Thus, one could say that this section is about "straightening out" the heart by "straightening out" the body, in the sense of doing required or recommended good deeds, and guarding the body from performing evil actions. Omitted in the translation, the passage gives the example of *facing* the direction of Mecca (the *qiblah*)—rather than any other direction—while praying, reciting litanies of remembrance, or performing ablutions. Just as the direction of the *qiblah* is preferred and ennobled by its purpose, and actions performed while facing it are considered sanctified, so too is the right side given preference to the left, because of the greater strength of the right hand over the left in most cases. Thus, cutting your fingernails starting from the right and then moving to the left is a form of beginning with the noblest side. Likewise, beginning with the right index finger is preferred owing to its special status of being the digit that you extend while declaring the Oneness of Allah. And so on. It is not about an obsessive compulsion toward stringent rules and micromanagement of every affair, but rather prioritizing your actions through beginning with the most noble, even in the most minute details.

107 The example used by al-Ghazali pertains to the ancient medical theory of humors. For example, experimentation may show that honey can be beneficial for a person who has a "cold temperament" or harmful to one who has a "hot temperament."

108 Al-Ghazali gives as examples, omitted from the translation, "your knowledge that following worldly desires ensures your heart's attachment to the worldly realm, or your knowledge that persistence in remembrance of Allah Most High assures intimate nearness [*al-uns*] to Him."

109 There may be other actions that impact the heart whose effects may not be known through experience or trial and error, but rather are known only by way of the Prophet's guidance.

The Secrets of Following the Example of the Prophet

Know that to mention each of the individual examples of the *sunnah* would be quite lengthy, this book being unable to contain all of them. It is necessary, however, that you know that they are reducible to three types of secrets:

1. The first pertains to the connection between the physical and the spiritual realms, between the limbs and the heart, and how the heart is influenced by the actions of the limbs. The heart is like a mirror, and the ultimate realities will not be manifested in it except through polishing, illumination, and rectification.

    As for the heart's polishing, it is through removing the impurities of base desires and the turbidity of blameworthy manners. Regarding the illumination of the heart, it is by way of the lights of remembrance and experiential knowledge. As for the heart's rectification, it is that all the movements of your limbs occur in accordance with the rules of uprightness.[106] The meaning of uprightness is putting everything in its place....

2. The second secret is that you know that those things that have an effect on your body, the cause for some of them is known to the intellect through their connection to heat, cold, moistness, and dryness....[107] Others are not known via analogy, ... but rather are known via inspiration or experience.... Likewise, the effects of actions on the heart are divided into those that are known via their relationship to it[108] ... and those not known via analogy, which are not known except by the light of prophecy.[109]

3. The third secret is that the felicity of a person is compared to the angels with regard to refraining from base desires, breaking the evil-commanding self, and being far from resembling unattended cattle that follow their caprice without restraint.

110 You do not reach heaven except through love and knowing Allah. You do not achieve love and knowledge except through constant reflection and remembrance of Allah. Owing to the importance of remembrance and prayer, al-Ghazali then recommends how you can organize your life around acts of worship.

111 Al-Ghazali mentions in *The Revival of the Religious Sciences* how you might go about doing this. You should repeat the common invocations, such as "There is no God but Allah," "Glory be to Allah," "All praise is due to Allah," "Allah is greatest," "There is no power or might except with Allah," and so on, from three to one hundred times. He also recommends reading certain chapters and verses of the Qur'an, as well as contemplating your past sins and seeking forgiveness for them. He also mentions specific invocations, prayers, and actions for each of the following times.

112 During this time, from when the sun has fully risen until just before noon, you should pray the additional recommended prayers associated with this time, as well as do good deeds and serve people. Al-Ghazali mentions visiting the sick, attending funeral prayers, doing good deeds, attending gatherings of the learned, and so on.

113 During this time, the noon and the afternoon prayers should be prayed, as well as the recommended (*sunnah*) prayers associated with them. It is an opportune time for supplication.

114 This is a time for glorifying Allah and engaging in remembrance, especially between the evening and the night prayers.

CONCLUSION

☐ Regarding the Ordering of Your Litanies That Incline You Toward These Ten Foundations...

It is necessary that you allot your time to various good deeds from your mornings to your evenings, and from your evenings to your mornings.

As you were taught before, what is sought from acts of worship is ensuring intimate nearness [to Allah] by way of remembrance of Allah Mighty and Majestic, for turning to the eternal abode, and withdrawing from the illusory abode.[110]

You should organize your litanies of remembrance and worship as follows:

1. From the time you awake from sleep until the rising of the sun, it is necessary that you combine in this noble time remembrance of Allah, supplication, reading the Qur'an, and contemplation.[111]

2. From sunrise to noon.[112]

3. From noon until sundown.[113]

4. From sundown until nightfall, and this is the most noble of times.[114]

(continued on page 111)

115 Such a person, however, should not leave the remembrance of Allah.

These are the recommended times for the worshipper. If you are a teacher, a student, or a ruler, occupying yourself with teaching, learning, or attending to the affairs of the people during the day is one of the best forms of worship of the body.

Likewise, if you are employed and are the breadwinner, establishing the rights of the dependents of your family through acquiring permissible goods is better than the superogatory forms of worship of the body.[115]

Here ends the section on the outward actions, and it is sufficient, Allah willing.

BOOK III

Purification
of the Heart

✧ Before the heart can be receptive to the ultimate spiritual realities, it must first be purified of the dross of worldly attachments and sin. The Qur'an extols spiritual purification (see 87:14 and 91:9). The Prophet, according to al-Tirmidhi and others, said, "Purification is half of faith." The business of purification of base traits, as well as the adornment of one's spiritual psychology with meritorious states, is the domain of *Ihsan*, or spiritual perfection. The science associated with *Ihsan* is called by different names, but the reality is one. In the West, it is often known as Sufism. What follows are the ten core base traits of which you must purify yourself.

1   The word *sharr* can be translated as "sin," "evil," "harm," "iniquity," and so on. Like many Arabic words, to capture its meaning in a single English word is often difficult. What is discussed in the following ten matters are things that are harmful spiritually, physically, and socially, as well as forbidden by Allah, and are therefore considered sins.

2   The logic here is similar to psychologist Abraham Maslow's hierarchy of needs, in that once you have satisfied your base physiological desires, you soon move on to desire an increase in wealth. Following soon after achieving wealth, al-Ghazali insists, often comes the love of rank in the eyes of others, followed by the rest of the blameworthy and ruinous traits.

3   There have been many rigorously authenticated hadiths narrated in a number of collections regarding the emphasis that Islam places on hunger as a means of breaking worldly attachments and desires. A common use of fasting is to curb sexual desire in unmarried men and women or, at minimum, to assist in self-restraint.

4   Suffering, especially the hardship of hunger, is one of the things that lead to paradise. Heaven is described as having different gates through which different people pass according to their merit.

☐ The Evils¹ Related to Food

Food is from the mothers of all evils....²

The Prophet said, "There is no action more beloved to Allah Most High than hunger and thirst."³

The Secret Regarding the Exaltation of Hunger

Perhaps you desire to know the secret regarding the exaltation of hunger and its relation to the path to the afterlife.

Know that there are many useful benefits, but they can return to seven core principles:

1. Purity of the heart and penetrating insight....

2. Softening and polishing of the heart until you perceive with it the joy of intimate discourse and the heart is affected by remembrance and worship....

3. Humbling the ego and the disappearance of pride and the ego's oppression. Nothing breaks the ego like hunger.

4. Tribulation is from among the doors of paradise.⁴ People do not have the power to punish their ego except with hunger.

5. Hunger is among the greatest benefits, as it breaks the rest of the base desires that are the origins of disobedience. It also conquers the evil-commanding self.

(continued on page 117)

5   Although it is not a requirement, the Prophet and those of his followers who strive to attain the higher ranks of worship and closeness to Allah would often wake in the latter part of the night to pray additional prayers called *tahajjud*, as mentioned previously. According to al-Ghazali, hunger lightens the body and makes it easier to wake up for these prayers. The root of excessive sleep that prevents you from waking up for these prayers, according to al-Ghazali, is eating too much.

6   Ibn Khaldun, the well-known fifteenth-century polymath, jurist, and historian, writes in his *Muqaddimah* that people can gradually decrease their food and water intake until they need very little to survive. However, to return to eating a normal amount after achieving this state could result in death, just as starvation would kill a person who is used to eating regularly. In any case, Sufism is not a do-it-yourself science, so you should not attempt the extreme measures mentioned by al-Ghazali.

7   That is, if you are willing to diminish the quantity of food that you eat, there are three things you must consider diminishing: how often you eat, how much you eat, and what you eat.

8   Since people are required to do more than merely stand, al-Ghazali's statement implies that, at this level, you eat only enough to perform daily rituals and work.

9   *Mudd* is equivalent to about 0.51 liter. The one at this level is content with about 0.25 liter of food a day.

10   The Prophet recommended that people devote a third of their stomach to food, a third to water, and a third to air. Some scholars have commented that "everyone knows his third." That is, a third may differ from person to person. A third of the stomach of a person who has gradually decreased intake of food is certainly not the same as that of a person who overeats.

6. Hunger lightens the body for night prayers and other worship.[5]

7. Lightening burdens, making possible contentment with few worldly goods and making possible preference for poverty, for one who rids himself of the sins of the stomach is not in need of much money.

Proceeding in Steps Regarding Decreasing Your Food

Perhaps you might say, "Eating one's fill and there being an abundance of food have become customary. How does one leave it?"

Know that leaving that is easy for a person who desires it, if done in degrees, decreasing your food each day by a morsel,[6] until you decrease by a loaf of bread in the span of a month....

If you concede to diminishing, you must consider it with regard to time, amount, and type.[7]

As for a decrease in amount, there are three degrees:

1. The first is the highest, and it is the rank of the truthful. It is to restrict yourself to the ability to stand. It is that you fear that to decrease from this amount would entail harm to your intellect or life.[8]

2. The second is that you are content with half a *mudd*[9] each day, amounting to a third of your stomach.[10] That was the norm for the Prophet's companion Umar and others.

3. The third is that you are content with one *mudd* per day.

(continued on page 119)

11   Going hungry does not imply eating or drinking absolutely nothing, though it may involve fasting during the daylight hours and eating and drinking very little at night.

12   Ibrahim ibn Adham was an eighth-century pious worshipper who is revered as an early exemplar of Sufi ethics and piety. Sufyan al-Thawri was an eighth-century scholar who had his own school of law, though it did not survive into the present day. He is also known for his piety, so it is not uncommon to reference him with regard to spiritual rather than purely legal matters.

13   The way of Sufism, especially in matters such as decreasing your food, traditionally should not be traveled except under the guidance of an experienced master. For some, decreasing their intake may help them on the spiritual path; for others, a balanced and non-gluttonous approach may be better.

14   Being on the Sufi path entails that you have made a commitment to purifying your soul of base traits, and attempting to adorn it with meritorious traits, through spiritual practices such as remembrance of Allah (*dhikr*) and other practices.

As for a decrease in time, there are also three degrees:

1. The highest is that you go hungry[11] for three days, or higher. Abu Bakr went hungry for six days. Ibrahim ibn Adham and al-Thawri[12] went hungry for seven. Others have gone for forty days. This is not possible except by decreasing your intake gradually.[13]

2. As for the middle degree, it is that you go hungry for two days.

3. The lowest is that you eat only once a day. As for the person who eats twice a day, he does not achieve the state of hunger.

As for a decrease in type:

The highest is to eat only wheat bread with some shortening, and its lowest is to eat barley bread without shortening....

As for those who are traveling the Sufi path,[14] they intensify this by leaving even the shortening; indeed, they do their utmost to leave all base desires.

15 Speech is especially powerful because it can both reflect and impact what is in the heart. So a person who is prone to lying imprints the form of those lies on his or her heart, twisting and distorting it. Likewise, a person who speaks excessively about superfluous things blackens his or her heart, until the spiritual heart eventually dies.

16 This hadith is narrated in the collection of al-Bukhari. It might be rendered that whoever keeps his speech in line with the sacred law and also avoids adultery and fornication is guaranteed salvation. These are two matters that many take lightly but are in fact considered of the utmost importance, because of the spiritual impact on the individual as well as the social impact on society.

THE SECOND FOUNDATION

☐ The Evils Related to Speech

It is necessary that you cease from these evils, for indeed all of the limbs' actions have an effect on the heart, but especially the tongue.[15] For this reason, the Prophet emphasizes the matter of the tongue, saying, "Whoever can guarantee what is between his two jawbones and his two legs, I guarantee heaven."[16]

The Evils of the Tongue

Know that there are twenty evils of the tongue, which we have explained in *The Revival of the Religious Sciences*, and their mention is a lengthy affair. However, it suffices you to act by the one verse of the Qur'an: "In most of their secret talks there is no good. But if one exhorts to a deed of charity or justice or conciliation between men, (secrecy is permissible). To him who does this, seeking the good pleasure of Allah, We shall soon give a reward of the highest (value)" [4:114]. The meaning of this verse is that you must not say what you do not mean and that you confine yourself to mentioning only those things that are important, for in this lies salvation.

17   The harm in lying would seem self-evident. Just as food is the source of love of wealth and rank, lying and falsehood can also lead to other blameworthy characteristics in a person, such as ostentation, discussed in a later chapter.

18   Both the hadith collectors al-Bukhari and Muslim ibn Hajjaj have narrated this hadith, considering it rigorously authenticated. Its meaning is that a person who tells an occasional lie and repents of it is not defined as a liar. However, a person who lies frequently eventually is considered a full-fledged liar and is judged by Allah as such. In other words, people are defined by the actions that they do frequently, not occasionally.

19   This may refer to the daughter of Abu Bakr, and sister of the Prophet's wife 'Aisha, who was a narrator of hadith. The Prophet also had a daughter named Umm Kulthum, and there was at least one other woman in the time of the Prophet or his companions named Umm Kulthum.

20   This hadith can be found in the collection of Muslim ibn Hajjaj, although with a slightly different wording in which the narrator mentions at the end, "and a man speaking with his wife, and she with him." Al-Ghazali explains elsewhere that when speaking is a means to achieving a praiseworthy objective, if speaking the truth can achieve that objective, then lying is impermissible. If telling the truth cannot achieve the objective then lying is permitted—if the objective is permissible—and obligatory if the objective is obligatory.

Elaboration of Some of the Evils of the Tongue

Perhaps you want to know the details of some of the evils of the tongue, so know that of the twenty evils that occur, most often on people's tongues are these five: lying, backbiting, disputation, joking, and composing panegyrical poems.

The First Evil: Lying[17]

The Prophet said, "A person continues to lie until he is written with Allah as a liar."[18]

WHEN IS LYING PERMITTED AS A DISPENSATION?

Know that lying is forbidden with regard to everything except by extreme necessity.

Umm Kulthum[19] said, "The Prophet did not permit any dispensations with regard to lying except in three matters: a man who says something untrue desiring mending relations, a man who says something untrue in war, and a man speaking with his wife."[20]

(continued on page 125)

21   Backbiting (*ghibah*) is likened to eating the flesh of your dead brother, a horrifying and revulsive comparison for something that is commonplace in everyday conversation.

22   Backbiting can include making a grimace at the speech or actions of another behind the person's back, making a gesture with your hand, imitating the person's speech or demeanor, or some other means that expresses a meaning that would offend the person.

23   The headings for each of these six exceptions are borrowed from the writings of al-Nawawi, as translated by Nuh Keller, in his *Reliance of the Traveler: The Classic Manual of Islamic Sacred Law Umdat Al-Salik* (Beltsville, MD: Amana Publications, 1997).

24   If the sultan, that is, the one possessing power of leadership, appointed a governor to rule over a particular area, and the governor turned out to be an oppressor, the people would be well within their rights to mention this oppression to the sultan, who could relieve the oppressive governor from his post.

25   When asking an opinion from a person who is qualified both to explain what Islam teaches about a given matter and to tell an individual in a specific situation how to apply this teaching, it is permissible to mention another's faults, seeking advice. For example, a person might ask, "My neighbor has done such and such. Has he wronged me?" Or, as in the Prophet's time, a woman might seek advice, saying, "My husband is stingy." However, it is still religiously more precautionary to phrase your questions generally, in order to avoid exposing another's faults, such as "What do you think of the case of a woman whose husband is stingy?"

26   When asked about a person's character for the purpose of determining whether that person is a suitable husband for the inquirer's daughter, it would be permissible to mention a negative trait that might negatively impact the daughter's life. For example, if the potential husband were an abusive alcoholic, it would be permissible, indeed necessary, to mention this fact.

The Second Evil: Backbiting

Allah Most High says in the Qur'an, "Would any of you like to eat the flesh of his dead brother? Nay, ye would abhor it.... But fear Allah. For Allah is Oft-Returning, Most Merciful" [49:12].**21**

Know that the definition of backbiting, as the Prophet has explained, is that you mention about your brother something that he would dislike if it reached him, regardless of whether you mention a flaw in his person, intellect, clothes, actions, speech, house, lineage, riding animal, or any other thing connected to him. Backbiting is not limited to the tongue alone; rather, there is no difference if you say it or indicate it.**22**

WHEN IS BACKBITING PERMITTED AS A DISPENSATION?

1. Redressing Grievances:**23** Such as when a person who is oppressed mentions the oppression of the oppressor to a leader**24** in order to rid himself of the oppression. As for mentioning it to someone who lacks the ability to deflect the oppression from him, in that case it is not permissible.

2. Eliminating Wrongdoing: When a person is seeking assistance in changing a wrongdoing, it is also permitted that he mention the matter to the sultan (or someone who can assist him).

3. Asking for a Legal Opinion: A person who is seeking a legal opinion may mention something otherwise considered backbiting if the question requires it.**25**

4. Warning Muslims of Evil: A person may mention something that would otherwise be considered backbiting to a Muslim in order to warn him of the evil of another.**26**

5. Identification: A person may mention something that would otherwise be considered backbiting if that person is known by a name that implies a defect, such as "the bleary eyed" or "the lame," though it is better to forgo such a term in preference of another that does not mention a deficiency.

(continued on page 127)

27   One of the punishments for backbiting is that your own good deeds are transferred to the person you backbite. On the Day of Judgment, as mentioned above, people's deeds will be weighed on a scale. If the bad deeds outweigh the good deeds, you suffer the punishments of hell. Thus, you should follow up a bad deed with a good deed, to try to balance out the scale, and refrain from transferring your good deeds to another's account through backbiting.

28   Others have disagreed with al-Ghazali, saying that repentance from backbiting is sufficient if you ask Allah for forgiveness, especially if alerting the victim to the slander might cause more harm than good.

29   This hadith has been narrated by al-Tirmidhi and Ibn Majah, though the wording in this text varies a bit from other recensions. The meanings, however, are the same. What is meant by disputation, as the scholar al-Nahlawi explains, is picking apart someone's words in order to find a mistake in it, whether grammatically, in meaning, or in intention. This is only when doing so is motivated by contempt or showing off. As for disputing with someone in order to make the truth known from falsehood, it is better to remain silent if the matter is a neutral matter, unconnected with religion, rather than get into debate. However, if the matter is related to religion, such as correcting misconceptions about your faith or correcting a misquoted saying of the Prophet, then you are obligated to openly correct the falsehood. (See related sections in *Reliance of the Traveler*.)

30   Pleiades is a distant cluster of stars that is mentioned here and elsewhere implying something at a great distance. This hadith has been authentically narrated by Ibn Abi Dunya and by others as well.

31   One example of the Prophet's joking is when he said to an elderly person, "The elderly do not enter heaven." What was understood from this was not that if a person lives to old age she will not enter heaven, but rather she will be resurrected in a younger form, according to some sources in the form of a person in her early thirties.

6. Someone Unconcerned with Concealing His Disobedience: As for a person who is unconcerned with concealing his fault and is not offended by its mention—such as the owner of a brothel.

Curing the Ego from Backbiting

The cure for the ego with regard to restraining it from backbiting is to think about the promises and threats that have been narrated by the Prophet regarding the punishments for backbiting.[27] If you backbite, you must seek forgiveness from Allah Most High, and then go to the one whom you have slandered and say, "I have oppressed you, so forgive me."[28]

The Third Evil: Disputing and Debating

The Prophet said, "Whoever forgoes disputation—when he is in the right—a house will be built for him in the highest part of heaven, and whoever forgoes disputation—when he is in the wrong—a house will be built for him on the edge of heaven."[29]

The Fourth Evil: Wrongful Joking

Excessive joking increases immoderate laughter, kills the heart, causes resentment, and eliminates your dignity and reserve. The Prophet said, "Verily a man says a word that causes those present to laugh, and by this word he falls further than Pleiades."[30]

Know that a little joking from time to time is permissible, especially with women and children in a way that is pleasing to their hearts. This has been transmitted from the messenger of Allah; however, he said, "Indeed I tell jokes, but I do not speak anything except the truth," and he urged others to do just that.[31]

32   Panegyric poetry refers to poems praising a person, often a king or wealthy person. As discussed in what follows, not all panegyrics are forbidden, as long as they do not include impermissible content or lead to impermissible things.

33   The four evils associated with panegyric poets are (1) going to excess in praise, until you lie; (2) displaying love that you do not actually feel, thereby being hypocritical; (3) becoming reckless in your praise, saying things that you have not verified; and (4) causing the one praised to rejoice when the one praised is a grave sinner and oppressor—such a person should not be praised, but rather condemned. The two evils associated with the one praised are (1) that you may thereby become proud and conceited, and these are two very destructive qualities; and (2) that you rejoice in the praise and become complacent in your actions, being pleased with yourself.

34   That is, if the poems and their effects are free of the six evils previously mentioned, then your act of composing such poetry might merit reward from Allah. Indeed, there is a long tradition of composing panegyrics about the Prophet. Also, the Prophet used to praise different people, such as praising his companion Abu Bakr for his faith, though not in poetic form.

The Fifth Evil: Composing Panegyric Poetry

Composing panegyric poetry[32] in the way that is customary for those who visit worldly kings and nobles, and as the storytellers do, indeed they praise the rich people who attend their gatherings.

There are six evils associated with composing panegyrics, four associated with the poets and two with the one being praised.[33] If the panagyric is free of these evils, composing such poems and lyrics is permissible, and possibly meritorious.[34]

35   As hinted at below, there are at least two types of anger. One is for the sake of Allah, and this is good anger, which can be channeled into positive actions. The other is bad anger, which is for the sake of your ego and attributed to the devil. Therefore, you must put out the fire of bad anger, or else you have embraced the devil's inherent nature.

36   This hadith has been narrated by both al-Bukhari and Muslim ibn Hajjaj. Often a person who manifests his strength outwardly by knocking others down (literally "causing one's adversaries to prostrate") is viewed as *al-shadid*, a word implying strength and harshness. However, the Prophet reminds us that the inner battle against the ego is greater than the outward battle against another person, and especially so when controlling your anger. Indeed, uncontrolled anger often leads to dangerous and terrible results.

37   This hadith has been narrated by al-Bukhari. The Prophet's repetition of this advice indicates the importance of controlling your anger. Inwardly and outwardly, anger carries negative qualities and consequences.

THE THIRD FOUNDATION

☐ Anger

Know that anger[35] is a flame of fire, lit from Allah's fire, that overtakes hearts. Whoever it overcomes has inclined toward the hereditary disposition of the devil, for indeed he was created from fire.

Breaking the power of anger is among the most important aspects of religion.

The Prophet said, "The strong person is not the one who causes his adversaries to fall; rather, the strong person is the one who controls himself when angry."[36]

A man said to the messenger of Allah, "Advise me." The Prophet responded, "Don't get angry." The man asked him again several times; each time the Prophet responded, "Don't get angry."[37]

38 In the technical terminology of the Sufis, spiritual training (*riyadah*) has been defined in several ways. It generally refers to living an austere life, disciplining yourself through limiting your carnal desires such as food, drink, and sleep, to what facilitates and promotes remembrance of Allah and other praiseworthy actions and states.

39 Anger is a weapon in that it will motivate you to stand up to attacks on your beliefs, person, and lands by hostile foes bent on destroying you and your religion. It is important to note that al-Ghazali does not categorize all disbelievers as hostile enemies, as he recognizes elsewhere that there are those who have not been reached by the message of Islam, those who do not attack the believers, and those who are protected minorities under Islamic law.

40 Anger is like a hunting dog that does not oppose the hunter who trained it. Anger is led, like a hunting dog, by the intellect and sacred law, abiding by their guidance. This is only possible after a great deal of spiritual struggle against the self and becoming habituated to forbearance and resisting those things that cause anger.

41 These various actions indicate that humbling yourself and lowering yourself (as in sitting or lying down) play a part in breaking your pride, and indeed pride is a major component in the anger that is forbidden by sacred law.

Curing Anger

You have two tasks with regard to the attribute of anger:

1. The first is breaking it [anger] by spiritual training.[38] By "breaking it," I do not intend "removing it," for indeed its root does not disappear, and it is not necessary that it disappear; indeed, if it disappears, it is necessary to obtain it, because it is a weapon against the disbelievers,[39] a preventer of bad deeds, and a multiplier of good deeds....[40]

2. The second task is restraining anger when enraged, by concealing your anger and keeping silent.

There are two prescriptions, one related to knowledge and the other to action:

1. As for knowledge, it is that you know there is no cause for your anger except the denial that a thing occurs by the will of Allah rather than by your own will; this is the utmost limit of ignorance.

   The other is that you know that the anger of Allah upon you is greater than your own anger, and that the grace of Allah is greater....

2. As for action, it is that you say, "I seek refuge in Allah from the accursed devil" if you know that the matter is from the devil. If your anger does not subside, you should sit if standing, and lie down if sitting—as it has been narrated in various hadiths—for the change in positions will cause your anger to subside. If it does not subside, you should do your ablutions.[41]

42   While this chapter of the Qur'an was not cited by al-Ghazali in the original text, it has been added here because of its relevance. This is one of two short chapters of the Qur'an recited for protection from various evils, including the evil of envy [113:1–5].

43   This hadith has been narrated by Abu Dawud with what scholars of hadith call a weak chain of narration, that is, this hadith does not reach a level of surety that can be claimed with confidence that the Prophet said it. However, al-Khatib al-Baghdadi, an eleventh-century scholar of hadith from the city of Baghdad, narrates it with a sound chain, meaning of greater surety that the Prophet said it.

44   *Ni'mah*, translated here as "blessing," refers to any good and pleasing object or state that is granted by Allah.

45   The word "envy" in English can have multiple connotations. We can say, with regard to the Arabic terms here, that there are two types of envy:

1. *Hasad* means you covet what another has and hope that the other will lose it or will be afflicted with a misfortune.

2. *Munafisah* means you covet what another has but do not hope the other will lose it or be afflicted with a misfortune.

THE FOURTH FOUNDATION

☐ Envy

Allah Most High says in the Qur'an:

Say: "I seek refuge with the Lord of the Dawn
From the mischief of created things;
From the mischief of Darkness as it overspreads;
From the mischief of those who practice secret arts;
And from the mischief of the envious one as he practices envy."[42]

The Prophet said, "Envy eats good deeds just as fire consumes firewood."[43]

Know that envy is forbidden. It is that you would like that a blessing[44] be removed from someone else or that you would like that a misfortune descend upon him.

Rivalry is not forbidden. Rivalry is that you envy[45] someone and desire the same for yourself without wanting the blessing to be removed from him.

It is permissible that you would like a blessing to be removed from a person who acquired it by oppression and sin, for you do not thereby desire the removal of blessings, but rather you desire the removal of oppression. The sign of this sort of desire is that if the person in question left oppression and sin, you would not desire the removal of the blessing.

The cause of envy is either pride, enmity, or having a wicked self, in that you are stingy with a blessing of Allah upon His servants without there being any objective for you in it [to obtain thereby].

46   Likewise, envy multiplies the good deeds (*hasanat*) of your enemy, because envy entails the transfer of your good deeds to the one you envy, even more so when envy is coupled with *ghibah* (backbiting). As the envier, you seek the removal of worldly blessing from your enemy, but you ironically end up assigning to him more blessings of the after-life and obtain for yourself the punishments in the world and in the afterlife. Al-Ghazali compares the envier to one who pelts his enemies with stones but misses them, and the stones return and hit him in the eye, blinding him, and increasing the malicious joy of the ultimate enemy, the devil.

47   You oppose envy and do the opposite of envy, by praising your enemy, manifesting happiness with your enemy's blessings, and so on.

Curing Envy

Know that envy is one of the major diseases of the heart, and the disease of the heart is not cured except by the medicine of both knowledge and action.

As for the knowledge cure: it is that you know that your envy harms only yourself and does not harm the one you envy; rather, it benefits him. As for it harming yourself, it is that it nullifies your good deeds and exposes you to the wrath of Allah Most High, for you are discontent with divine destiny and are stingy with Allah's blessings that He has generously bestowed upon His servants from His storehouse. This is the harm to the envier's religious life.

As for the harm to your worldly life, it is that you do not cease to be in constant sorrow and inescapable grief, which is what your enemy desires for you. Among the most important objectives of your enemy and the most perfect of your enemy's blessings is the sorrow of his envier, for you the envier had wanted a tribulation to befall your enemy, but obtained it for yourself instead.

The envious one is never devoid of grief and affliction, since your enemy's blessings are not removed. As to the fact that envy benefits your enemy without harming him, it is because the blessing does not disappear by way of the envier's envy....[46]

As for the action cure: it is that you know the ruling for envy and that which it necessitates with regard to speech and action. So you oppose it and act according to its opposite,[47] extolling the one you envy, manifesting joy at the blessings bestowed upon him, and behaving humbly toward him. With that, the one envied returns to you as a friend, and envy departs from you, and you are rid of its evil and suffering.

Allah Most High says in the Qur'an, "Nor can goodness and evil be equal. Repel (evil) with what is better. Then will he between whom and thee was hatred become as it were thy friend and intimate!" [41:34].

48 That is, you do not say or do anything that would manifest your envy; rather, you oppose the inclination to do so.

49 However, your natural disposition can be conquered, such as by regarding only Allah and turning away from the world and other people. Such a person knows that Allah is the bestower of all blessings and that these blessings in the world could not benefit a person if he were in hell and would be of little regard for a person who is in heaven. That is to say, a nice job and a fancy car can do the denizens of hell no good and are of no interest to the people of heaven, where the blessings are far greater than those they experienced in the world.

How to Be Rid of the Sin of Envy

Perhaps your ego does not comply with your wishes with regard to considering your friends and enemies equal; rather, you dislike harming of a friend, to the exclusion of an enemy, and you like that a friend receive blessings to the exclusion of an enemy, such that you say, "I am not held responsible for that of which I am not capable," so if you are not able to do that, then you must be rid of the evil by way of two matters:

1. The first is that you do not manifest envy on your tongue, limbs, or voluntary actions; rather, you oppose that to which they call you.[48]

2. The second is that you dislike in yourself its desire for the removal of Allah's blessings from one of His servants. If the religiously motivated consideration (of the desire) as being reprehensible is combined with the desire for the removal of blessings that are necessitated by natural disposition, the sin is repelled from you, and you need not change the disposition, for indeed you are not capable of that in most states.

    The sign of dislike is that you are at the point where, if you had the ability to remove a blessing from another, you would not endeavor to remove the blessing despite wanting it to happen; if you had the ability to assist him in perpetuating or increasing the blessing, you would do that despite disliking doing so. If you are as such, then there is no sin upon you in that which your nature necessitates.[49]

50   This hadith is narrated by al-Nasa'i and others narrators of hadith. I have included it in the main text because it is sounder, although al-Ghazali included a less authentic hadith of similar meaning.

THE FIFTH FOUNDATION

☐ Stinginess and Love of Wealth

Know that stinginess is from among the major destructive evils.

Allah Most High says in the Qur'an, "But those who before them, had homes (in Medina) and had adopted the Faith, show their affection to such as came to them for refuge, and entertain no desire in their hearts for things given to the (latter), but give them preference over themselves, even though poverty was their (own lot). And those saved from the covetousness of their own souls, they are the ones that achieve prosperity" [59:9].

Allah also says, "And let not those who covetously withhold of the gifts that Allah hath given them of His Grace think that it is good for them. Nay, it will be the worse for them: soon shall the things that they covetously withheld be tied to their necks like a twisted collar, on the Day of Judgment. To Allah belongs the heritage of the heavens and the earth; and Allah is well acquainted with all that ye do" [3:180].

The Prophet said, "Miserliness and Faith are never combined in the heart of one person."**50**

51   This hadith has been narrated with a rigorously authenticated chain by Ahmad ibn Hanbal and al-Tabarani.

The Root of Stinginess Is Love of Wealth

Know that the root of stinginess is love of wealth, which is blameworthy. A person who does not have money, his stinginess is not made apparent by its being withheld from him, but rather by his love of wealth. Many a man is generous, yet he loves wealth. So he is generous with it [his wealth] in order that he is called openhanded, and this too is blameworthy, because love of wealth diverts him from the remembrance of Allah Mighty and Majestic, and turns the face of the heart toward the world, and determines his relationship to it [the world], until death—in which there is the meeting of Allah Most High—becomes heavy and burdensome to him.

Allah Most High says in the Qur'an, "O ye who believe! Let not your riches or your children divert you from the remembrance of Allah. If any act thus, the loss is their own" [63:9].

He Most High also says, "And know ye that your possessions and your progeny are but a trial; and that it is Allah with whom lies your highest reward" [8:28].

He Most High also says, "The mutual rivalry for piling up (the good things of this world) diverts you (from the more serious things)" [102:1].

Wealth Is Not Blameworthy in Essence

Know that wealth is not blameworthy from every perspective. The messenger of Allah said, "How wonderful is virtuous wealth for the virtuous man!"[51] How can wealth be absolutely blameworthy when the servant is a traveler to Allah and the world is one of the way stations of his travels? [Furthermore, how can it be blameworthy when] his body is his riding mount, and it is not possible to travel to Allah without it?

(continued on page 145)

52   In this context, the provisions of a traveler are intended; a traveler takes only what he needs for the journey.

53   Despite being surrounded by permissible things, living a life of luxury can lead to negative habits, like relying on people for assistance and depending on oppressive and corrupt rulers. That, according to al-Ghazali, leads to hypocrisy, lying, ostentation, enmity, and hatred, and thereby ruin.

54   In the pursuit of acquiring more and more worldly things, and especially in competing with others for such worldly wealth, you forget Allah, and the ultimate goal of Muslim spiritual life.

55   The gold dinar was the standard currency in the Muslim world from the Prophet's time until the modern era, when gold and silver currency was replaced with paper money, and, recently, virtual money. The gold dinar, and its counterpart the silver dirham, are measured in weight, the dinar being about 0.125254 ounces of gold, and the dirham being about 3.207 ounces of silver. At the time of this writing, the dinar equaled about 300 U.S. dollars. Although other forms of currency existed, such as copper coins or even dinars and dirhams mixed with other metals, these gold- and silver-based coins maintained a certain stability throughout the ages.

56   In an age in which clothing is mass-produced in factories by machines and underpaid workers, where even on a very meager income a person can often obtain far more clothing than he or she needs, such an idea as al-Ghazali's is quite shocking, that is, owning just one or two *thawbs* (ankle-length shirts). However, in his time, clothing was handmade, from fabrics that were handwoven. Indeed, clothing was often stolen from travelers by highway bandits because of its high value.

The body does not subsist except by food and clothing, neither of which can be obtained without wealth. However, whoever understood the benefit of wealth and knew that it is a means of feeding one's riding animal for traveling the path, he did not stop at it nor did he take from it except to the extent of provisions,[52] and if he restricts himself to that he is happy with it.

If he exceeds the amount that suffices him, he is destroyed....

Likewise the traveler, if he takes in excess of the provisions of the path, he dies under its weight, and he does not reach the destination of his travels.

Exceeding the amount that suffices is ruinous from three perspectives:

1. The first is that you are called to sin, as sin is made possible by wealth....

2. The second is that you are called to living a life of ease and comfort via the permissible....[53]

3. The third is that you are diverted from the remembrance of Allah Mighty and Majestic....[54]

The Amount of Wealth That Suffices

Perhaps you desire to know the amount that suffices one.... Know that the bare necessity is that you require only food and clothing. You abandon adorning yourself with fancy clothes and suffice yourself in the year with two dinars[55] for your winter and your summer, acquiring coarse clothes that repel the heat and the cold.[56]

(continued on page 147)

57   The Prophet recommended that you eat just enough to keep your spine straight, that is, just enough nutrition to keep the body functioning properly and remaining healthy. If you want to eat more, then he suggested that your stomach be filled one-third with food, one-third with water, and one-third with air.

58   *Mudd*, as mentioned previously, equals 0.51 liter. The gist is that you do not go to excess in fulfilling your needs. Al-Ghazali was writing in a time of great abundance in which, to use his words, "hearts had changed and become overcome with stinginess." In a time of such abundance, it may be better to withdraw from it all and live a simple and austere life. However, such a lifestyle is not for all travelers of the Sufi path. Indeed, one person may be better off earning a living through work rather than devoted to superogatory worship, while another may be better off living a life of utter simplicity and devoted to worship.

59   This advice is for the one who busies himself with worship. The seeker of knowledge, on the other hand, spends his time studying. While the amount that suffices may differ from person to person, depending on the individual, if you seek beyond what suffices, then you are considered to be from among the people of worldliness (*ahl dunya*). The gist is that if you spend all your time seeking more and more wealth, your ability to do things that benefit your soul in this life and the next decreases. If you busy yourself with earning money in order to support good causes, give in charity, and spend your wealth in the way of Allah, you can find your spiritual benefits even in your buying and selling. The ideal is not that your hand be empty, but rather that your heart be empty of what is in your hand.

60   One who is determined does not find hardship in hunger, as he knows that it leads to greater happiness in the afterlife.

Also, you abandon luxury in your food and satiation[57] from food in all of your states and suffice yourself each day with a *mudd*....[58]

... So, acquire in a day what you need for a day, and withdraw [from worldly affairs] and busy yourself with your worship....[59]

Wealth Is Like Medication

What has been mentioned above is approximate; it is possible that it increases or decreases according to the interpretation and deduction of various individuals and in various states. However, such individuals believe absolutely that wealth is like medication, and the beneficial from it is a specific amount, and the excess in it is deadly, and approaching excess causes sickness if not death. Therefore you must strive to approximate from the amount that is necessary, and to be wary of excess and luxury, for that is a major peril.

There is nothing in a decrease in wealth except a little difficulty in the days of scarcity. For you who possesses determination, it is not heavy upon you that you cause your self to go hungry....[60]

61   Often translated as "manliness," *maroo'ah* is akin to a code of chivalry that emphasizes generosity. It has also been translated as "kindness."

62   One who avoids stinginess to the degree necessitated by Islamic law is not considered stingy, though, according to al-Ghazali, he is not thereby considered generous and benevolent. Furthermore, you do not attain the rank of "generous and benevolent" by merely avoiding stinginess as necessitated by *maroo'ah*. You must exceed these two stages in order to be truly generous, that is, you must spend well beyond the compulsory and what kindness dictates. See *The Revival of the Religious Sciences*, "Book 27: Condemnation of Miserliness and Condemnation of the Love of Wealth" for more details.

63   Al-Ghazali mentions in *The Revival of the Religious Sciences* that the cure to every disease is found in the application of its opposite to the root cause of illness. Patience and satisfaction with few worldly goods oppose greed. Awareness of the inevitability of death treats the disease of procrastination and having long hopes. Stinginess is cured through knowing its evil nature and the rewards of charity and generosity. Forcing your hand to give in charity is the action-cure that opposes and treats stinginess, as discussed below.

64   An electuary is a medicinal paste.

65   You might begin by tricking yourself by reaping the benefits of being openhanded, that is, by gaining a good name for your generosity and thereby desiring to be generous, not for the meritorious reason of giving for the sake of Allah but rather for the blameworthy praise of people. Once you have become openhanded, albeit for the wrong reason, you can then work on ridding yourself of the negative trait of seeking praise. This is basically an example of doing a lesser evil to bring about a positive effect and then ridding yourself of the lesser evil once the positive effect is in place. Naturally, such an approach can only be taken with knowledge of the sacred law and is not to be taken lightly.

Definition of Stinginess

Perhaps you wish to know the definition of stinginess, when you might doubt whether or not a particular individual is stingy, and the people disagree with regard to him.

Know that the definition of stinginess is: holding back from that which the sacred law or chivalrous generosity[61] necessitates.[62]

Curing Stinginess[63]

Perhaps you want to understand the cure to stinginess. Know that its cure is an electuary,[64] composed of both knowledge and action.

Regarding knowledge: It is that you know what stinginess contains of destructive things with regard to the afterlife and what it contains of blameworthy things in the *dunya*. It is also that you know that wealth does not follow you—if it remains—to the grave. Moreover, wealth belongs to Allah Most High; He places it in your hands in order that you spend it on the most pertinent of your affairs.

As for action: It is that you make yourself spend freely, against your nature, and you do not cease to do that until it becomes customary for you.[65]

66   The term *hubb al-jah* implies fame and prestige not just in the sense of being well known, but also in the sense of being in a position of high rank and power. Henceforth, it will be translated as "prestige," with the abovementioned implications.

67   This hadith has been narrated by both al-Tirmidhi and al-Nasa'i, with slightly different wordings.

68   This hadith has been narrated in the collection of al-Daylami, with a weak chain of narration, meaning that it cannot be attributed to the Prophet with a high degree of surety. Al-Daylami refers to a twelfth-century scholar of hadith or to his son, both of whom narrated hadiths, some of which were of questionable authenticity. Despite the lack of surety in attributing the text to the Prophet, the meaning is sufficiently in line with Islamic teachings.

69   The righteous caliphs (*al-khulafa' al-rashidun*) are the four companions of the Prophet—Abu Bakr, Umar, Uthman, and Ali—who served as leaders of the Muslim community after the Prophet's death. In addition to these companions, scholars such as Egyptian scholar Jalal al-Din al-Suyuti (d. 1505) have argued that the Prophet's grandson Hasan is also included among the righteous caliphs, because he ruled for six months before acquiescing power to the Prophet's companion, Mu'awiyyah. With Mu'awiyyah's reign, the era of the righteous caliphs came to a close, and thus began a period of hereditary rule and, eventually, competing empires from varying familial or sectarian backgrounds.

THE SIXTH FOUNDATION

☐ Frivolity and Love of Prestige[66]

Allah Most High says in the Qur'an, "That home of the hereafter We shall give to those who intend not high-handedness or mischief on earth; and the end is (best) for the righteous" [28:83].

The Prophet said, "Two hungry wolves sent amidst a herd of sheep are not as mischievous and harmful as the love of wealth and prestige are to one's religion."[67]

The Prophet said, "The love of wealth and prestige sprouts hypocrisy from the heart, as water causes herbs to grow."[68]

From this you know the blameworthiness of fame and prestige, except when Allah makes a person famous in religious matters without seeking it from Him, as He made the prophets, righteous caliphs,[69] scholars, and saints famous.

The Reality of Prestige Is Possessing Hearts

The reality of prestige is the possession of hearts in order that they be subjugated to the will of the one endowed with prestige, that they cause the tongue to speak his praises, and that they pursue his needs.

Just as the meaning of "wealth" is the possession of money by which a person obtains his aims, likewise the meaning of "prestige" is the possession of hearts. Prestige, however, is more beloved, because by it wealth is obtained more easily than prestige is achieved by wealth....

(continued on page 153)

70 Omitted in the translation and summarized here is the argument al-Ghazali gives that by seeking fame, grandeur, magnificence, and majesty, a human being is ultimately seeking to rival Allah in His absolute independence and omnipotence. Becuase all things are ontologically dependent on Allah's power, it is said that they have no real, independent existence; they are "a shadow from the light of Allah's power," and therefore Allah is the only independent and truly existent being. When you seek rank and authority, it is as though you seek to be the central focus, to be one without partner, but this position is only for Allah. The quintessential case of a person who was so desirous of fame and rank that he claimed divinity for himself was Pharaoh, who, despite claiming himself "your lord most high," was swallowed up by the Red Sea after Moses led his people out of Egypt (see Qur'an 29:15–74).

When you leave this ultimately delusional state, you may still seek mastery over everything, but through knowledge. You desire to know all the marvels of the universe, from the planets and the heavens, to the mines beneath the mountains and the pearls at the bottom of the sea. When you reach this state, your bestial inclinations lessen, and your lordly attributes predominate; that is, your desire for knowledge causes your intellectual faculties to strengthen and take precedence over your physical desires.

71 Despite the potentially beneficial outcome of seeking rank and perfection through seeking knowledge of the marvels of the universe, you might wonder why the pursuit of rank and perfection is blameworthy. Al-Ghazali explains, in a passage omitted from the translation, that it is only blameworthy when accompanied by blameworthy motives. If all that is sought is nearness to Allah, then seeking rank and perfection is considered meritorious. When sought for blameworthy purposes, it is called "delusional rank and perfection." When sought in order to achieve nearness to Allah, it is called "true rank and perfection."

There is another secret related to prestige, and it is that the meaning of prestige is grandeur, magnificence, and majesty, these being attributes of the Divine and beloved to the human being by nature; indeed, it is the sweetest of things with him....**70**

High Rank and Perfection

Know that seeking the truly high rank is praiseworthy, not blameworthy, when what is universally sought is nearness to Allah Most High....**71**

(continued on page 155)

72   Beneficial knowledge (*'ilm*) and being free of attachment to all created things (*hurriyyah*) are states that benefit you even after death, as discussed below. Coupled with the recognition that all things in the universe are created by Allah's infinite power (*qudrah*), true perfection is attained.

73   That is, you are able to get things done because you possess wealth and fame.

74   True perfection attributes power to Allah, whereas delusional perfection attributes power to the individual. But the reality is, the person has no real power, just that which comes from having high fame, prestige, and great wealth. Recent history, such as the ongoing "Arab Spring" at the time of this writing, sufficiently illustrates how the loss of rank with the people can lead to a leader's demise, despite having control over lots of money.

75   That is, freedom is separating your attachment to all that does not follow you to the grave. You take with you to the grave your knowledge, states, good deeds, and the perpetual rewards of lasting charity and the prayers of those left behind. From another angle, freedom is separating from all that is of no benefit to your afterlife.

76   Although neither wealth nor children are in and of themselves bad, excessive focus on them leads to misplaced focus, thereby forgetting Allah and your ultimate spiritual goal.

77   Those who suffered a loss—translated here as "the unfortunate"— have it backwards. They coveted that which had no benefit, and they turned their backs on that which has lasting benefit.

Rather, what is blameworthy is seeking delusive perfection to the exclusion of true perfection, which goes back to knowledge, freedom, and power.[72] It [true perfection] is that it not be tied to other than Him, and the servant is not conceived of as possessing the reality of power, for indeed his power is only by wealth and prestige,[73] which is delusional perfection, for indeed it is an accidental property that does not abide, and there is no good to be found in that which does not abide.[74]

Rather, perfection is in those enduring righteous things by which nearness to Allah is obtained, Glorified is He. These do not end with death; rather, they multiply without limit, and that is the true experiential knowledge of the entity of Allah Most High, and His attributes, and His actions.

Freedom is included in true perfection. Freedom is severing your connection from all worldly connections, indeed from all that is separated from you at death,[75] and limiting yourself to having regard for He who of necessity does not leave you, namely, Allah Most High....

Knowledge and freedom are among the lasting righteous things, and they are two true perfections. Wealth and children are ornaments of the life of the world, and they are two delusional perfections.[76]

The unfortunate—that is, those who reverse the ultimate reality,[77] are averse to seeking true perfection, and busy themselves with seeking delusional perfection—are those who are consumed by the fires of grief at death when they witness that they have forfeited their *dunya* and afterlife.

(continued on page 157)

78 A person who knows Allah experientially and is free of attachment to worldly things finds piety and devotion to Allah pleasurable and thereby increases those actions and spiritual states that lead to salvation.

79 Al-Ghazali refers to one's inheritors as enemies metaphorically, in reference to the common scenario of relatives of the deceased squabbling over what remains of wealth.

80 That is, at the time of the resurrection and Day of Judgment.

81 To summarize the previous section, seeking high rank and perfection is not blameworthy if they are connected to the ultimate reality (i.e., Allah). True high rank is achieved when what is sought is nearness to Allah. Blameworthy rank is when you seek delusional perfection, instead of the perfection associated with the ultimate reality that returns to knowledge, freedom, and power. Delusional perfection is when you believe that your ability to get what you want is real, when in fact it stems from fame and rank, which depends on others. These two attributes are accidental properties; they do not subsist or last forever. Whatever is temporary has no good in it. Rather, what is good is what lasts forever. What lasts forever are knowledge, spiritual states, good deeds, and so on, as these benefit you after death. Indeed, when we die, we take our knowledge and spiritual states with us to the grave. The best knowledge is the experiential knowledge of Allah (gnosis), and this multiplies without limit after death.

82 You, your fame, and the people who admire you are all in a state of perishing; none remain on the earth more than a century or so, but more often less than that. Even if your fame lives on, it does you no benefit, unless by it a good aim is achieved (i.e., beneficial knowledge is transmitted or people continue to pray for you). Allah, however, is eternal and never perishes, and His judgment of you will have a far greater impact on your eternity than the judgment of human beings, who are His servants under His command and are only in existence temporarily. They have no power over you ultimately, nor over your life, death, earnings, and so on.

As for losing their afterlife, it is because they did not seek nor obtain its means via gnosis and freedom.[78]

As for losing their worldly life, it is because it bids them farewell at death and is transferred over to their enemies, that is, their inheritors.[79]

Do not suppose that belief and knowledge depart from you with death, for death by no means demolishes the locus of knowledge. Death is not nonexistence such that you would think that if you are nonexistent, your attributes are nonexistent.

Rather, the meaning of death is "severing the connection of the soul to the body, until that time when it returns to it."[80] When it is denuded of the body, the soul is as it was before death with regard to knowledge and ignorance. The comprehension of this is a lengthy matter, and under it are many secrets the revelation of which this book could not carry.[81]

Preventing Love of Fame

If you know the reality of fame and its fundamental nature and that it is a delusional perfection, then you know that the way of curing yourself of it is by preventing the love of it from entering the heart.

For example, if you know the people of the earth, if they prostrated to you, neither the one prostrating nor the one to whom they prostrate would remain in existence, except for a brief moment.[82]

83   Praise makes you feel good because it assumes a position of influence and control over the one offering the praise.

84   The more you are praised by people, the more your fame spreads. The spread of your fame then leads to even more praise. This in turn leads to more fame, and the cycle repeats. The spread of fame also leads to power and possibly wealth.

85   Praise from the spiritually insightful feels good because the one who is praising you is held in high regard. If a wise man calls you wise, you are likely to feel happy about this. If the praise comes from those who are not insightful, it falls flat. It is like a fool calling you a wise man.

86   That is, 1–3 above.

87   The study of the metaphysical writings of the ancient Greek philosophers and their followers is considered by al-Ghazali to be a sinful and risky pursuit, as the doctrines espoused in such writings are largely conjectural and often lead to denial of fundamental religious truths. Contrary to popular opinion in the Western academic discourse, this condemnation of the metaphysical sciences did not entail the end of critical thinking or the rational sciences, because al-Ghazali was a strong proponent of the science of logic, which he considered to be a religiously neutral science that was highly recommended for any legal or theological scholar. See his *Deliverance from Error* for a detailed discussion of his views on the various sciences (*Deliverance from Error: Five Key Texts Including His Spiritual Autobiography, al-Munqidh min al-Dalal*, trans. R. J. McCarthy [Louisville, KY: Fons Vitae, 1999]).

88   You should be saddened by praise, not gladdened, if the praise is for something fleeting, like wealth or fame. As mentioned in al-Ghazali's first angle for delighting in praise, praise causes its possessor to perceive his self's perfection, which is delusional, because perfection is for Allah alone.

Motives for Seeking Prestige

Among the motives for seeking prestige is the love of praise, for indeed the person is delighted by praise from three angles:

1. The first is that praise causes its possessor to perceive his self's perfection, and the feeling of perfection is sweet, because perfection is from the attributes of divinity.

2. The second is that praise informs [its possessor] of the possession of the heart of the one praising him and of having prestige in his eyes and his being subjected to him.[83]

3. The third is that praise makes its possessor feel that the one praising him inclines toward praising him and his fame will thereby spread.[84]

The first delight of praise ceases when it originates from other than the people of insight, for indeed it does not make one feel perfection.[85]

The second delight of praise ceases when it originates from someone lowly and vile who possesses no standing or rank, because the possession of his heart is insignificant.

The third delight of praise ceases when he is praised in private, not publicly, except from the perspective that he anticipates that the one praising him might also praise him publicly.

As for dispraise, one dislikes it due to its contradicting these afore-mentioned causes.[86] Most people are destroyed by their love of praise and dislike of dispraise, making them pursue ostentation and the study of sinful sciences.[87]

The cure for that is that one think about the first delight, and if he was praised for having lots of wealth and fame, then he knows that it is a delusional perfection, and that it is the cause of the lapsing of true perfection. It is appropriate that he is saddened on account of it, not that he rejoices at it.[88]

89   Such a person does not consider these pious traits to come from his own efforts; rather, he considers them a gift or a blessing from Allah. Proper etiquette with Allah is that you attribute the good to Him, and the bad to yourself.

90   Such a person is like one who feels complimented by someone commenting on how pleasant the scent of his cologne is when in fact he is not wearing any cologne, and it is rather the scent of the person sitting next to him. To be gladdened by such a comment is sheer foolishness.

If he was praised for the perfection of knowledge and scrupulousness, it is necessary that his happiness is due to the existence of these attributes, and he thanks Allah Most High for them, not others.[89] This is if he actually possesses these attributes. For if he is not described by these attributes, then his happiness with such praise is foolishness....[90]

As for the second and third delights ... their cures are what we have mentioned earlier with regard to the love of prestige.

91 Because of the subtle implications of the word *dunya*, or "worldly concerns," and the incompleteness of the English term "world," it has been left untranslated throughout much of this chapter. The *dunya* is not merely the universe and everything in it. Rather, it is everything that pleases the self and does not lead to merit in the afterlife. Therefore, a successful career in medicine, for example, might be an example of your *dunya* if your intent and goal are merely to get rich. However, the same career can be considered an act of worship if done for the sake of Allah, intending to serve humanity and to fulfill a communal obligation (*fard/kifayah*).

92 There are different aspects of the *dunya*—some external and physical, some internal. In other words, there is an inner *dunya* and an outer *dunya*, the former referring to our attachments to physical matters of this world without benefit in the next world, and the latter referring to inner ruinous traits such as pride and envy. Al-Ghazali explains, in a passage summarized here and omitted from the translation, that there are physical things of the world that test a person's spiritual focus and resolve. See Qur'an 18:7.

Among these are land for residence and cultivation, vegetation for medicinal and nourishing foods, and minerals for currency (i.e., gold and silver), vessels (i.e., silverware, cups, pitchers, plates), and tools (i.e., plows, swords, shovels). Other examples include animals for riding (i.e., horses, camels, donkeys) or eating, and human beings for marriage, family, interacting, and so on. This is summed up in Qur'an 3:14.

As for seeking your portion of these physical worldly things, it is considered a base desire if you seek beyond what is needed to worship and serve Allah (see Qur'an 79:40 and 57:20).

THE SEVENTH FOUNDATION

☐ Love of the World

Know that the love of the world[91] is the head of all transgression. The *dunya* is not only equivalent to wealth and fame. Rather, wealth and fame are two sins from among the many sins of the *dunya*, and two of its branches, of which there are many.

Your *dunya* is equivalent to your state before death, and your afterlife is equivalent to your state after death.

Everything that you possess of it before death, it is from your *dunya*, except knowledge, gnosis, and freedom. Whatever remains with you after death, it is also a delight with the people of spiritual insights; however, it is not *of* the *dunya* even if it was *in* the *dunya*....[92]

(continued on page 165)

93 Indeed, seeking worldly things leads to the inner ruinous traits (*al-mahlukat al-batinah*): malice, pride, envy, ostentation, hypocrisy, boasting, excessive amassing of wealth, love of the *dunya*, and love of praise. These ruinous spiritual/psychological traits are described by al-Ghazali as the inner *dunya*, while the corporeal things of the earth are the outer *dunya*. Attachments to the outer *dunya* lead to increase in your inner *dunya*.

As for seeking to better your worldly position via the generality of occupations, trades, and the industries with which people busy themselves, this causes people to forget themselves in their work; they forget their ultimate beginning and destination through absorption in working for that to which their hearts are connected.

94 A *ribat* can refer to a place of rest built for travelers along the roadside or to a guard station on the outlying borders of a nation that houses guards engaged in austere living, extensive worship, and recollection (*dhikr*) of Allah. Both meanings seem to fit al-Ghazali's intent, though perhaps the former is more fitting.

95 The people of the *dunya* are like the passengers on a tour boat who take too long to explore the sites at an uninhabited island. Too caught up in exploring the island, smelling the flowers, and marveling at the landscape, their ship leaves, and they are left to fend for themselves against the hardships of survival.

This is the reality of the *dunya*, love of which is the head of all transgression.[93] Moreover, it was created in order to obtain provisions [in the journey] toward the afterlife. However, excessive preoccupation with it and the varieties of its desires cause the foolish to forget their journey and their aim, and they confine their aspirations to it. They are like the pilgrims in the desert who became so preoccupied with attending to the she-camel, feeding it and fattening it, that they fell behind from the group until they missed the pilgrimage altogether and were killed by the desert lions.

The *Dunya* Is a Cultivated Field of the Afterlife

This very same blameworthy and destructive *dunya* is also a cultivated field of the afterlife with regard to one who knows it, when he knows that it is one of the way stations of the traveler to Allah Mighty and Majestic; it is like a hostel or guard station[94] that is built on the roadways, preparing in it feed [for one's riding animals], provisions, and the means of travel. So whoever takes provisions from it [the *dunya*] for his afterlife and limits himself in what he takes from it to only the amount necessary—as we mentioned regarding food, clothes, marriage, and the rest of the necessities—he has cultivated and sowed the seeds, and he will reap what he sowed in the afterlife. Whoever turned toward it [the *dunya*] and busied himself with its delights is destroyed....[95]

96   The people of spiritual insight know the truth through direct experience.

97   *Taqlid* is to follow another's opinion without knowing the evidence for it. What is implied is that you are following the reasoned and researched opinion of another despite your not having done the background research nor contemplated the issue sufficiently. In modern terms, it is similar to your following a medical doctor's advice without questioning it or with only a nonspecialist's degree of independent research. *Taqlid* in matters of belief is generally not permissible; a person's faith must be built on a personal affirmation. However, al-Ghazali's intent may be that a person who is sufficiently grounded in his or her faith but does not have faith based on personal spiritual experience should trust the advice of those who are more grounded through their having experiential knowledge of Allah (i.e., gnosis).

98   This has been authentically narrated by Ibn Majah and al-Tirmidhi. In the terminology of hadith scholars, its chain of narration is sound (*hasan*).

The Enmity of the *Dunya* for the Afterlife

Whoever knows himself, his Lord, the ornaments of the *dunya*, and the afterlife witnesses with the light of spiritual insight the enmity of the *dunya* for the afterlife, when it is decidedly disclosed to him that there is no felicity in the afterlife except for one who reaches Allah knowing Him and loving Him. Indeed, love is not bestowed except by persistent remembrance, and gnosis is not granted except by perpetual seeking and meditative contemplation. A person does not devote himself to love and gnosis except one who is averse to worldly activities. Gnosis and love do not take possession of the heart that is not rid of love of other than Allah Most High. Emptying the heart of other than Allah necessarily entails busying it with the love of Allah Most High and gnosis; that is not conceivable except by being devoid of the *dunya*, satisfied from it with the amount sufficient for provisions and necessity. If you were from the people of spiritual insight, then you would have become from among the people of tasting and witnessing.[96] If you are not like that, then be from among the people who follow[97] others in faith, and look to the warnings of Allah—Glorified is He—to you in the Qur'an and Prophet's sayings. Allah Most High says in the Qur'an, "Those who desire the life of the present and its glitter, to them we shall pay (the price of) their deeds therein, without diminution" [11:15].

Allah Most High also says, "This is because they love the life of this world better than the hereafter; and Allah will not guide those who reject Faith" [16:107]. He—Mighty is His Name—also says, "Then, for such as had transgressed all bounds, and had preferred the life of this world, the Abode will be Hell-Fire" [79:37–38]. Perhaps a third of the Qur'an is about dispraising the *dunya* and its folk.

The Prophet said, "The *dunya* and all that is in it is cursed, except for that which is for Allah Most High...."[98]

99 Claiming to be "in it but not of it" is delusional, because it is impossible not to be affected, even if minimally, by your surroundings.

100 This hadith has been narrated by Ibn Abi Dunya, a ninth-century scholar of hadith from Baghdad, and by al-Bayhaqi.

101 Such a person is like one who checks into a hotel for a night and becomes attached to the furniture, television, and other accoutrements, despite knowing that after checking out they will no longer be his to use. Worldly possessions are loaned as hospitality for the traveler, not given for permanent ownership.

Whoever Closely Associates Physically with the World, His Heart Is Not Devoid of It

Know that whoever thinks that he can closely associate with the world physically while his heart is devoid of it is deluded.[99] The Prophet said, "The worldly person is like the one who walks in water; is it possible that he walks in water and his feet do not get wet?"[100]

Know that whoever feels secure in the *dunya* while believing with certainty that he is departing from it is in the utmost extremes of stupidity....[101]

Indeed the *dunya* is an abode of Allah's hospitality for those passing through—not for those residing in it—in order that they might take as provisions from it that which benefits one, just as a loaned item is benefitted from, then left with a pure self and unattached heart to whoever arrives after one.

102 The terms "haughtiness," "pride," and "arrogance" are all synonyms in English and have a negative connotation, but the term *al kibriya'* when applied to Allah has the implication of grandeur and majesty, not an unwarranted pride.

103 This hadith has been narrated by Ibn Majah, Ibn Hibban—a tenth-century scholar of hadith—and Abu Dawud, with similar wordings. It has also been narrated in a different form by Muslim ibn Hajjaj. This is a type of hadith called a *hadith qudsi*, wherein the wording is the Prophet's, but the meaning is Allah's; that is, the Prophet chooses the words to express a meaning that Allah has communicated to him. It is different from the Qur'an, because the Qur'an comprises both Allah's words and Allah's meanings.

104 This hadith has been narrated by Muslim ibn Hajjaj. In its full form, it also includes the definition of arrogance (*kibr*) as being "denying the truth and having contempt for people." See Abdul Hamid Siddiqi's translation of Muslim ibn Hajjaj's "Sahih Muslim" online, book 1, chapter 40: www.usc.edu/schools/college/crcc/engagement/resources/texts/muslim/hadith/muslim.

THE EIGHTH FOUNDATION

☐ Arrogance

Allah, glorified is He, says in the Qur'an, "(Such) as dispute about the signs of Allah, without any authority that hath reached them, grievous and odious (is such conduct) in the sight of Allah and of the believers. Thus does Allah seal up every heart of arrogant and obstinate transgressors" [40:35].

Allah Most High also says, "Enter ye the gates of Hell, to dwell therein; and evil is (this) abode of the arrogant!" [40:76].

The Prophet said, "Allah Most High said, 'Grandeur[102] is My cloak, and Might is My robe, and whoever competes with Me in either of them I shall break him.'"[103]

The Prophet said, "No one will enter paradise who has a mustard seed's weight of arrogance in his heart."[104]

105 The wording of this hadith is taken from the version narrated by Muslim ibn Hajjaj and quoted in the previous annotation. The version al-Ghazali uses in the text has the same meaning but has a slightly different wording. I have chosen to use Muslim ibn Hajjaj's rather than al-Ghazali's wording because of the greater authenticity of the former's narration. Al-Ghazali did not cite the hadiths he mentioned, and at times, the wordings differ from the standard versions. At other times, he combines the meanings of two hadiths into one, while at other times, it was not possible for later hadith scholars to locate the source of some of the hadiths he attributes to the Prophet. For this reason, some scholars of hadith have criticized al-Ghazali.

The Reality of Arrogance

The reality of arrogance is that you see yourself as being superior to others in possessing attributes of perfection. So there occurs in you haughtiness and a delightful sensation from this view and belief....

Then external actions proceed from this haughtiness, such as raising yourself up when in a gathering, and putting yourself forward in the path, and looking with the eye of contempt and anger when not greeted first,... and looking at the common masses as if they were donkeys. Moreover, arrogance is considered such an enormity that you do not enter heaven if you have an atom's weight of it [arrogance] in your heart, because there are three classes of major evils associated with arrogance:

1. The first evil is that you are contending with Allah Most High with regard to the exclusivity of His attribute, since Grandeur is His cloak, as Allah has said [in the abovementioned hadith]. Indeed, might is not befitting except for Allah. From where does might befit the lowly servant that does not own anything from his own affair, let alone the affair of another?

2. The second evil is that arrogance attributes to you the denial of truth and disdain for the people. The Prophet said with regard to explaining arrogance, "Arrogance is denying the truth and having contempt for people."**105** Disdaining the truth closes the door of felicity, and likewise, so does being contemptuous of people....

3. The third evil is that arrogance bars you from the entirety of praiseworthy manners, because the proud person is not capable of loving for the people what he loves for himself. Nor is he capable of modesty, or leaving disdain, envy, or anger. Likewise, he is incapable of concealing rage, giving kindly counsel, or leaving ostentation.

    On the whole, there does not remain any bad trait except that the arrogant person is compelled to perpetrate it, and there does not remain any good trait except that he is compelled to leave it.

106   If you are arrogant and proud, you should remember that there are aspects of your body and human nature that are beyond your control and nothing to brag about. No matter how great a person was in life, no one would want to be around the corpse of such a person once it began to decompose.

107   Here, al-Ghazali is referring to the following passage from the Qur'an: "Has there not been over Man a long period of Time, when he was nothing—(not even) mentioned? Verily We created Man from a drop of mingled sperm, in order to try him: So We gave him (the gifts), of Hearing and Sight" [76:1–2].

108   No matter how high and mighty we perceive ourselves to be, we are still bound by the humbling demands of the body.

Curing Arrogance

The general cure for quelling the depravity of arrogance is that the person knows himself, that he began as a drop of foul sperm, and his end will be an impure and rotten corpse, and between these two states he is a carrier of feces.[106] The cure to arrogance is also that one understands what Allah Most High says in the Qur'an:

> From what stuff hath He created him?
> From a sperm-drop: He hath created him, and then mouldeth him in due proportions;
> Then doth He make His path smooth for him;
> Then He causeth him to die, and putteth him in his grave. [80:18–21]

So one should know that he was created from the mysterious concealment of nonexistence and that he was a thing not even mentioned.[107] There is nothing less than nonexistence. Then, he was created from earth, then from a drop of sperm, then from clot, then from an embryo that did not have hearing, sight, life, or power, and then those were created for him. After that, he is in a state of utmost deficiency with illnesses and diseases overwhelming him, and there differs within him natural dispositions that demolish each other. He falls ill, goes hungry, and becomes thirsty against his will. He wants to know something but is ignorant of it. He wants to forget something, yet he remembers it. He detests something, yet it benefits him. He desires something, but it harms him. He does not feel safe for a moment from having his soul, intellect, or health swiped away from him, or even one of his limbs. Then his end is death and facing the punishment and reckoning [of the afterlife]. If he is from the people of hellfire, then pigs are better than him. So from where is arrogance befitting him when he is a lowly owned slave, capable of nothing? Hasan al-Basri—Allah's mercy be upon him—said to some folks who swaggered while walking, "What is this walking for one in whose belly is excrement?" How is arrogance befitting for one who washes away feces twice a day with his hand, while carrying it perpetually?[108]

109 Thinking that your knowledge and learning puts you above others for any reason is delusional. For al-Ghazali, as stated in the original text and omitted from the translation, knowledge is "that by which one knows oneself and one's Lord, the perilous consequences of his end, and the proof of Allah Mighty and Majestic against him." Likewise, we do not know how our final state will be. Al-Ghazali reminds us of the case of Umar, the companion of the Prophet who was among the most hated enemies of the Muslims in the early days of Islam and then ended up being one of the greatest companions of the Prophet upon conversion. Likewise, a great scholar could apostatize before death.

110 An ignorant person who has been scrupulous in his actions and worships outwardly, but not inwardly, can become deluded into thinking that the events that happen to those around him are miracles induced by their presence and pious actions. This type of delusion can even lead to disbelief, because a person might begin to see himself as better than the prophets.

111 Most humans (other than Adam, Eve, and Jesus [upon them be peace]) come into being via the union of sperm and egg. If you follow your lineage back to the Prophet Adam, you see that he was created from dirt. Attributing your genealogy to semen and dirt, rather than a famous and pious ancestor, is a humbling cure to pride. This is, perhaps, similar to Abraham's humble pronouncement in Genesis 18:27, "I who am but dust and ashes."

A Detailed Discussion of Curing Arrogance

A more detailed explanation of curing arrogance comes from looking at those matters in which haughtiness is found, namely, the following four qualities:

1. This first is knowledge.... Scholars who are devoid of the plague of arrogance have become scarce. Indeed an arrogant scholar sees himself as being above the people with regard to knowledge, which is the most noble virtue with Allah Mighty and Majestic. Sometimes, he becomes arrogant with regard to religion such that he sees himself as being better than others with Allah Mighty and Majestic....[109]

2. The second is scrupulousness and worship, while the worshipper is not devoid of arrogance internally. Sometimes this stupidity leads some of them to believe that the people's misfortunes and joys are induced by way of their miracles....[110] The proper manner of the true worshipper is that when he looks to the scholar he humbles himself to him due to his own ignorance. His duty is that if he looks to the grave sinner, he says, "Perhaps there is within him an inner trait that is hidden by his outward sins, and perhaps within me is envy, ostentation, or some concealed wickedness and Allah will detest me because of it and He will not accept my outward actions. [He must know] that Allah—Glorified is He—looks to the hearts, not the outward forms, and that among the inner wicked traits is arrogance."

3. The third is arrogance in lineage, and its cure is to look at one's lineage, indeed his father is a drop of semen, and his grandfather is dirt.[111] There is nothing filthier than semen, and nothing lower than dirt.

(continued on page 179)

112 Wealth can easily be stolen, followers are easily usurped by others, and beauty fades with time or scarring from disease or accident. These are temporary and external matters, and not significant enough on which to base your self-worth.

4. The fourth is arrogance in wealth, beauty, and followers. Arrogance in these is ignorance, for indeed they are matters that are external to one's essence. That is, wealth and followers, how can one be arrogant in these issues that are reached by the outstretched hand of the thief and the usurper?! Furthermore, how is one proud of a beauty that can be spoiled by a month's fever and caused to vanish by smallpox?...[112]

113 The word translated here as "elated" is derived from the same root as *'ujb* and thus has an added meaning of vanity, pride, and conceit.

114 Bashir ibn Mansur (d. 824–25 CE) was a man known for his deep commitment to worship.

115 Iblis, the devil, was an avid worshipper of Allah for thousands of years, but when Allah created Adam (upon him be peace), Iblis became proud and said, "I am better than he: Thou didst create me from fire, and him from clay" [Qur'an 7:12]. In a moment of proto-racism, his arrogance caused him to fall from being the best worshipper to the accursed devil who leads people to hell.

THE NINTH FOUNDATION

□ Pride

Allah Most High says in the Qur'an, "Assuredly, Allah did help you in many battlefields and on the day of Hunain: Behold! Your great numbers elated[113] you, but they availed you naught; the land, for all that it is wide, did constrain you, and ye turned back in retreat" [9:25]. He Most High also says, [Say: "Shall we not tell you of ...] those whose efforts have been wasted in this life, while they thought that they were acquiring good by their works?" They are those who deny the Signs of their Lord and the fact of their having to meet Him (in the hereafter): vain will be their works, not shall We, on the Day of Judgment, give them any weight [18:104–105].

He Most High also says, "... Therefore justify not yourselves: He knows best who it is that guards against evil" [53:32].

A man watched Bashir ibn Mansur[114] while he made his prayers lengthy and perfected his worship. When he finished, he said, "Do not be misled by what you have seen from me, for indeed Iblis worshipped Allah Most High and prayed for thousands of years, then what happened to him happened."[115]

116 Al-Ghazali did not mention a source for this narration, and efforts of later scholars to determine its source have not yielded evidence of its attribution to the Prophet or anyone else for that matter, but it has been included here to clarify the rest of the passage. Its meaning is in line with Islamic principles, even if its origin cannot be ascertained with certainty.

117 You will know you are conceited if you are surprised that your prayers are not answered or that your enemy experiences prosperity, financially or otherwise. Such a person mistakenly assumes that his high rank with Allah should entail his prayers being answered and his enemies being deprived of blessings.

118 The difference between pride ('ujb) and arrogance (kibr) is that arrogance implies seeing yourself as superior to another, whereas pride is seeing yourself as great without comparing yourself to another.

119 The proper etiquette with Allah is that you ascribe all blessings to Him and all shortcomings to yourself. The person who sees the blessings that Allah has bestowed upon him as being the result of his own efforts, but nonetheless realizes that Allah can remove these blessings at any time, is not guilty of pride; rather, he is guilty of bad etiquette.

120 The words "pride" and "admire" have the same root in Arabic, the former implying self-admiration, as opposed to the admiration of another.

121 Al-Ghazali asks us to consider: If a king gave you the key to his treasure, and you opened the vault and took from it, would you be amazed by the generosity of the king who gave you the key without your deserving it, or would you be amazed by your skill in using the key and taking the treasure? What sort of skill is entailed by doing something that another has enabled you to do? Therefore, our physical actions, for example, are not something to take pride in, for Allah has given us our bodies and can take them away at any moment.

The Reality of Pride

The reality of pride is that a person reckons himself and his various qualities to be great—which are from among the blessings of Allah—and then feels confident in them while forgetting to ascribe them to the Benefactor, while feeling secure against their disappearance. If he adds to this that he sees that his self has a portion and dignified rank with Allah, that is called conceit. It has been narrated that "the ritual prayer of the conceited does not rise above his head."[116] The sign of his conceitedness is that he is astonished by the rejection of his supplication and by the integrity of the state of one who harms him.[117]

Pride is the cause of arrogance; however, arrogance necessitates that there is someone over whom you feel arrogantly superior, while pride is conceived in isolation.[118] As for one who sees the blessings Allah bestowed upon him, such as an action, knowledge, or otherwise, while he is afraid of its disappearance, and rejoices at the blessing of Allah upon him in as far as they are from Allah Most High, then this is not pride; rather, pride is that one feels secure [against their disappearance] and forgets to ascribe them to the Benefactor [Allah].[119]

Curing Pride

Pride is pure ignorance, so its cure is pure knowledge. If he is proud of power, beauty, or an affair that is not connected to his own power, then he is also ignorant, for that is not attributable to him. So, he should admire[120] the One who gave him that without his deserving it. Also, he should keep in mind that the removal of that is to be imminently feared because of the slightest illness and weakness.

If he is proud of his knowledge, actions, and that which he does by his own volition, he should keep in mind that by which those actions are facilitated for him. Indeed, those actions are not made possible except by a limb, ability, will, and knowledge, and all of that is from the creation of Allah Mighty and Majestic.[121]

122 If a person has been given X, there is no rational reason that he also deserves Y. If a person is given a horse by the king, and another is given a servant, it is foolish to ask why someone else was given a servant and not a horse, while he was given a horse and not a servant. A king can give whatever gifts he desires to whomever he wants. Allah, as the ultimate King, can give whatever He wills to anyone He wills.

Knowledge and Intellect Are Gifts from Allah

It is amazing that an intelligent person would be proud of his knowledge and intellect, to the extent that he is amazed if Allah Most High has impoverished him and enriched some of the ignorant folk. So he says, "Why did He generously give blessings to the ignorant one and keep it from me?" So it is said to him, "How did he provide you with knowledge and intellect and keep it from the ignorant one? This is a gift from Him. Did you make it a cause for deserving another gift? Rather, if He gave you both intellect and richness, and forbade the ignorant one from them both, that would be more deserving of amazement...." Such a person has made a gift from Allah a reason for another gift, and this is the essence of ignorance.[122]

Rather, the intelligent one is always amazed by the grace and generosity of Allah Most High with regard to His giving him knowledge and intellect without his first having deserved it, while He deprived someone else of it....

123 This hadith has been rigorously authenticated and narrated in varying forms but with the same basic meaning in the collections of Malik, Muslim ibn Hajjaj, and Ibn Majah. In the language of hadith scholars, it is rigorously authenticated (*sahih*).

124 The Arabic term *riya'*, translated here as "ostentation," is derived from the word *ru'ya*, which means "seeing." Ostentation is doing an act of worship in hopes of being seen (and held in high esteem) by other than Allah, and is therefore the opposite of sincerity (*ikhlas*). Sincerity is doing an act of worship solely for the sake of Allah. This is why acts of worship, such as charitable giving, are sometimes best done privately, for fear of being *seen* by other people and falling into ostentation.

125 For example, a person might make himself thin and pale so that people might think he keeps long night vigils in prayer or that he fasts often. Another example is that a person manifests sadness so that people might think he is very concerned with religious matters. While it may seem strange in the modern world that one would seek status with people through such matters, in premodern times the religious people were often like the rock stars of today. If a person was very knowledgeable in religious matters, he might be rewarded with a high post in the government and thereby make large sums of money. Another might feign poverty and piety in order to draw a large following of disciples who serve him and give him gifts.

126 This differs from place to place and in different times. In al-Ghazali's time and place, such things as shaving the mustache, bowing one's head while walking, and closing one's eyes in such a way that others would think the person was in a state of spiritual ecstasy were pertinent examples of seeking a status with others through one's outward appearance.

THE TENTH FOUNDATION

☐ Ostentation

Allah Most High says in the Qur'an:

So woe to the worshippers
Who are neglectful of their prayers,
Those who (want but) to be seen (of men). [107:4–6]

The Prophet said, "Allah Most High says, 'Whoever performs an action for Me wherein others are associated with Me, such a person is left entirely to the one he associates with Me, and I am the most Self-sufficient and free of any association.'"123

The Reality of Ostentation124

The reality of ostentation is seeking a high status in the hearts of the people with acts of worship and good deeds.

That by which a person acts with ostentation are six categories:

1. The first is ostentation by way of the body.125

2. The second is ostentation in appearance.126

(continued on page 189)

127 Ostentation in clothing manifests in different ways, in accordance with whom one is hoping to achieve a high status. For example, a person might wear a coarse woolen garment and carry a large string of prayer beads so that people think he is an abstinent Sufi, or wear a headdress usually associated with scholars.

128 Those who are experts in public speaking, sermonizing in particular, might fall into this. Also, al-Ghazali gives as examples relating instructive stories or narrations from pious forefathers in a soft delicate voice, manifesting sorrow while inwardly being devoid of truthfulness and sincerity.

129 The ritual prayer (salah) is one of the primary contexts in which a person might manifest ostentation through action. When a person knows others are watching, he might lengthen the time that he stands and recites, or he might embellish his bowing and prostration. When he is alone, however, he might pray quickly and infrequently. But when he feels that someone might be watching, he returns to calmness and slowness in prayer or changes something in his outward demeanor outside of prayer so that people might think he is especially pious.

130 Having a large entourage of "yes-men," that is, those who agree with and support you at all times, is another sign of ostentation if building the large entourage is for the sake of achieving a high status in the hearts of people. If it is to spread the truth and focus on educating a future generation of scholars for the sake of Allah, then it is not blameworthy. Likewise, a person who mentions famous scholars so that people think he may have studied with them—that is, name-dropping—is also engaging in a form of ostentation particular to scholars and students of sacred knowledge.

3. The third is ostentation in clothing.[127]

4. The fourth is ostentation in speech.[128]

5. The fifth is ostentation in action.[129]

6. The sixth is ostentation in having many students and companions, and in frequent mention of scholars.[130]

All of the above examples of ostentation in matters of religion are forbidden; indeed they are from the major sins.

(continued on page 191)

131 This is a slippery slope, as seeking a high station in the eyes of others through these worldly means could easily lead to pride, arrogance, and other ruinous and blameworthy traits. Perhaps what is intended is that seeking rank with others in matters not connected to worship and piety is not in and of itself forbidden if your intentions are to obtain a permissible ends. For example, if you published a book of poetry to raise money for an orphanage, it would be permissible for you to promote the book, find other poets to praise your work, hire a publicist to promote your book and name, and so on if doing so were viewed as a tool for increasing the amount raised for the orphanage. If promoting your name and work were just for the sake of seeking a high station in the eyes of others, it might not be in and of itself impermissible, though it could easily lead to the impermissible.

132 This sort of ostentation could lead you into forbidden actions, since possessing the hearts of many people is like possessing a lot of wealth in that both could cause you to leave the remembrance of Allah (*dhikr*), that is, become forgetful of Allah, and thereby fall into sin. However, it is likely warned against for this potential, not for being bad in and of itself.

133 If you give money to a group of people in hopes that they will view you as being generous, but the money is in fact a debt you owe to them, then this is a form of deceit, and attempting to possess the hearts of people by way of deception is forbidden, even if you are not seeking a reputation for being pious.

As for seeking status in the hearts of the people by way of actions that are not matters of worship and religious actions, then that in which there is no deceit is not forbidden, as we mentioned in the section on seeking prestige. Indeed, the people of the *dunya* might seek a station with a lot of wealth, servants, and luxurious clothes, or by memorizing poetry, or by [learning] medicine, accounting, grammar, linguistic sciences, or other than that from actions and states....[131]

Moreover, we will examine the divisions of ostentation because it is the most dominant of blameworthy character traits upon people's egos. Whoever does not know evil and the contexts in which it occurs, it is not possible that he can be wary of it....

The Degrees of Ostentation

There are numerous ruinous degrees of ostentation. One of them is that it is not from matters of religion and worship, such as the person who wears fine clothes while out and about that differ from what he wears when alone.

Or like the person who spends lavishly on entertaining guests or spends on the wealthy in order that people believe he is generous, not in order that they believe that he is piously cautious and righteous, and this is not forbidden....[132]

As for manifesting the aforementioned character traits so that the people believe these traits are from the religion and from scrupulousness, they are forbidden for two reasons:

1. The first is that it is a deception if he desires that the people believe him to be a sincere person, lovingly obedient to Allah. A person with such an intention is a gross sinner and detested by Allah Most High.... Seeking to possess people's hearts by way of deception is forbidden.[133]

(continued on page 193)

134 This sort of deception is also a form of mockery. It is like one who offers his service to the king, outwardly appearing to be serving the king, but inwardly seeking the attention of one of the king's servants. Such a deception mocks the king, who thinks he is being served when in fact he is being used. A king is more powerful than his servants, so seeking the servants' attention and favor is absurd. Likewise, worshipping Allah hoping to benefit from one of His servants is even more absurd, because harm or blessings occur only by Allah's will. Ostentation is therefore considered a minor form of polytheism, because it attributes power and ability to other than Allah. Another form of ostentation that mocks Allah is the ostentation of those who use their acts of worship as a means of disobeying Him, such as establishing a charitable trust for orphans in order to squander their money.

135 An example of such a person is one who agrees to have an orphan's wealth deposited with him for safekeeping, but really intends to squander the deposit or, worse yet, spend it on impermissible things.

136 The *munafiq* is one who outwardly professes Islam, usually for some worldly or deceitful purpose, yet inwardly does not believe.

2. The second is that if he intends by his worship of Allah something
    of Allah's creation, then he is one who mocks.[134]

Among the ostentatious are those who do not seek anything except
pure prestige....

If a person makes his worship of Allah Most High a means to
opposing Him, this is the worst type of ostentation.[135]

By What Is Ostentation Obtained?

Just as the enormity of ostentation and the grossness of its sinfulness is
due to the differing motives spurring a person on, it is also due to those
matters on account of which he is ostentatious, as well as the strength
of his intention to be ostentatious.

Matters in which ostentation is found are of three degrees:

1. The grossest of which is that a person is ostentatious in the root
    of faith, such as the hypocrite[136] who outwardly manifests that
    he is Muslim, but he has not submitted in his heart.

2. The second is ostentation in core acts of worship, such as a
    person who prays and distributes the poor tax to the people,
    while Allah knows from that which is concealed in his inner self
    that if he were left to himself, he would not do those things.

(continued on page 195)

137 That is, a person who is not ostentatious in the five daily prayers, fasting during Ramadan, paying the poor tax (zakah), going on the pilgrimage to Mecca, and the like. This is opposed to a person who is ostentatious in the recommended, though not obligatory, acts of worship, such as additional prayers, fasting on days outside of Ramadan, giving voluntary charity, going on the pilgrimage a second time, and so on.

138 I understand from this to mean a person who might pay the poor tax (zakah) due on his livestock with the healthiest and most robust of his livestock or with the purest and highest quality of his food with regard to the poor tax due on his stored staple foods. Al-Ghazali assumes his reader is familiar with the fact that the poor tax is due on stored monetary wealth, certain types of livestock, staple foods, business merchandise, and buried treasure.

139 These are optional fasts that a person does for extra credit, so to speak. The former refers to fasting on one of the days of the Hajj ritual, and the latter refers to fasting on the tenth day of the Islamic month of Muharram in honor of the Prophet Moses and his people's deliverance from Egypt.

140 Such a scenario entails that the person's act of worship is hoped to be valid and rewarded, though he may be punished for the intention of ostentation, or perhaps, if not punished, then the reward might decrease.

141 In this scenario, the person's intention is equally for worship and ostentation, in which case there is disagreement between different Muslim scholars over whether the person will be punished for equally being ostentatious and intending worship. One opinion is that the two intentions cancel each other out, such that the act of worship is not valid or rewarded. In such a case, some scholars might argue that the intention for worship serves as an expiation for the sin of ostentation. However, according to al-Ghazali, despite the cancellation of intentions, it may still be sinful and punishable.

WIN A $100 GIFT CERTIFICATE!

Fill in this card and
mail it to us—
or fill it in **online** at
**skylightpaths.com/
feedback.html**

—to be eligible for a
$100 gift certificate for
SkyLight Paths books.

SKYLIGHT PATHS PUBLISHING
SUNSET FARM OFFICES RTE 4
PO BOX 237
WOODSTOCK VT 05091-0237

Place
Stamp
Here

Fill in this card and return it to us to be eligible for our quarterly drawing for a $100 gift certificate for SkyLight Paths books.

We hope that you will enjoy this book and find it useful in enriching your life.

Book title: _____

Your comments: _____

How you learned of this book: _____

If purchased: Bookseller _____ City _____ State _____

Please send me a free SkyLight Paths Publishing catalog. I am interested in: (check all that apply)

1. ❏ Spirituality
2. ❏ Mysticism/Kabbalah
3. ❏ Philosophy/Theology

4. ❏ Spiritual Texts
5. ❏ Religious Traditions (Which ones?)
6. ❏ Children's Books

7. ❏ Prayer/Worship
8. ❏ Meditation
9. ❏ Interfaith Resources

Name (PRINT) _____

Street _____

City _____ State _____ Zip _____

E-MAIL (FOR SPECIAL OFFERS ONLY) _____

Please send a SkyLight Paths Publishing catalog to my friend:

Name (PRINT) _____

Street _____

City _____ State _____ Zip _____

SKYLIGHT PATHS® Publishing   Tel: (802) 457-4000 • Fax: (802) 457-4004

Available at better booksellers. Visit us online at www.skylightpaths.com

3. The third and least is that a person is not ostentatious in the obligatory matters,[137] but rather, is ostentatious in the superogatory matters, such as one who prays a lot of superogatory prayers, and perfects the form of the obligatory actions, distributes the poor tax from the best of his wealth,[138] or prays the superogatory prayers in the last part of the night, and fasts the superogatory fasts of the Day of 'Arafah and 'Aashura',[139] while Allah knows from his inner self that if he were left to himself he would not do anything from these. This too is forbidden....

As for his going to the utmost degree with regard to the degrees of intention, it is that his ostentatious intention may become so absolute such that he prays, for example, without having done the ritual ablutions for the sake of people, or he fasts even though he would eat if he were by himself.

He might also annex to it the intention of worship, and for such a person there are three states:

1. The first is that the intention of the act of worship is independently impelling him and if he were by himself, he would still perform it. However, being seen by others increases the vigor with which he does the act of worship, and he fears over the action because of this.[140]

2. The second is that the aim of worship is weak, such that if he were to be away from people, he would not assume the burden of worship. Such an intention does not make his worship valid, and the presence of the weak intention for worship does not negate from it the high degree of detestation.

3. The third is that the two intentions are equal such that neither one can independently cause him to do it if they were separate, or he does not set out to do it by the motivation of just one of them. Rather he sets out to do the action because of both of them.[141]

[142] The ostentation is not the motivating force for the action; however, ostentation increases the enthusiasm with which he performs an action he was already accustomed to engaging in.

[143] This sort of ostentation indicates that its possessor considers his actions a gift or blessing to the people, as though he expects their respect and reverence for his acts of worship.

Manifest and Hidden Ostentation

Know that some ostentation is manifest, while some of it is more hidden than the creeping of ants.

As for the manifest ostentation, it is that which incites to action such that without it the person would not desire to do the action.

More hidden than that is ostentation by which the person would not assume the burden of an act of worship; however, the action is made easier for him and causes his eagerness to increase, such as one who prays the [voluntary] night prayers every night, and if there is a guest with him, it increases his zeal to pray.**142**

A more hidden form of ostentation is that the person's eagerness does not increase, but if another is made aware of his night prayers before or after completing them, he is gladdened by this and he finds within himself high spirits. This indicates that the ostentation was hidden inside the heart, hiding the fire under the ashes....

Still more hidden is ostentation within a person who is not gladdened by others being apprised of his pious acts; however, he expects that he is greeted first and honored....**143** None are devoid of the likes of these hidden forms of ostentation—all of which are sins—except the truthful. It is feared that actions in which there are any of these types of ostentation will be thwarted and come to no avail....

On account of the hidden nature of the doors of ostentation, and the severity with which it seizes a person's inner self, the resolute are on guard against it, and fear for their acts of worship, and strive against their lower selves....

So, if you want salvation, strive in order that you view people as you do animals or children, such that you do not distinguish in your acts of worship between their presence or their absence, or their knowledge of your actions or their ignorance of them, and be content with Allah Most High's knowledge of them, and seek the reward from Him, for indeed He does not accept any except the pure and sincere....

144 If ostentation is the impetus for prayer, it invalidates the prayer. For example, if you do not pray if others are not around to see the act of ritual prayer, it is invalidated by your ostentatious intention.

145 If ostentation occurs once the prayer has commenced, it invalidates the prayer only if the occurrence of ostentation is what keeps you from breaking off your prayer and doing something else.

146 If ostentation occurs after you complete the prayer, it does not lead to the prayer's invalidation, but does entail sin. From the perspective of taking account of your actions, you still have the reward for the prayer, but you have added weight to the other side of the scale pans, so to speak, by adding bad actions. The punishment for such ostentation is commensurate with the extent of the intention.

147 Al-Ghazali describes love of praise in a passage omitted from the translation as follows: "It is like one who charges a rank of soldiers so that he is called a valiant hero, or one who makes his acts of worship known so that he is called pious. Its cure is what was mentioned with regard to the cure for love of prestige, namely, that you know that it is a delusive perfection, without any reality. Its cure regarding ostentation is specific, and it is that one acknowledges in himself that which is in it of detriment, for indeed if there is honey in which there is poison, even if it is sweet, it is easy to leave it." Furthermore, you should remind yourself of your shortcomings, and know that Allah's approval and acceptance of your acts of worship are all that matter.

148 You should remember that the censure of others will not harm you if Allah Mighty and Majestic is pleased with you. It suffices to know that if people knew of the ostentatious intention in your heart, then they would detest you.

149 As for being motivated by covetousness, it is repelled by knowing that it is a delusory matter and that it completely cuts you off from Allah's satisfaction.

Is it Possible to Rid Yourself of Hidden Ostentation?

Perhaps you might ask, "I am not able to rid myself from hidden ostentation as you have described it, even if I have the ability to rid myself of manifest ostentation. Is my worship valid nevertheless?"

Know that the occurrence of ostentation is either at the beginning of an action,[144] or while it endures,[145] or after it is completed.[146]

Curing Ostentation

If you know the reality of ostentation and the multitude of ways it enters upon a person, then you must prepare yourself for the treatment for ostentation. Its cure is in repelling the three causes that motivate people toward ostentation, and they are:

1. Love of praise[147]
2. Fear of censure[148]
3. Covetousness[149]

150 In the terminology of the Sufis, attacks are states that enter your heart at a given moment, without any effort on the part of the individual. The power of the attack depends on the power of the situation. See al-Qushayri, *Al-Qushayri's Epistle on Sufism*, trans. Alexander D. Knysh, reviewed by Muhammad S. Eissa (Reading, UK: Garnet, 2007).

151 That is, such a person has his sights set on Allah and the afterlife, his heart disinclines from created things, and he is sincere. This is a sign of divinely granted success. Yet despite having broken any habits of ostentation and eliminated its root causes, there is still the possibility that he is occasionally attacked by ostentation, as if coming from outside his own nature and heart.

152 That is, upon an unexpected and unintended attack of ostentation when your act of worship is witnessed by another, you should call to mind that Allah detests ostentation, and remember that none can benefit or harm you except by Allah's permission.

153 The main thing that you are required to do is detest and resist the invitation to ostentation and thereby avoid falling into the sin of seeking status in the eyes of others through their witnessing or hearing of your acts of worship. As for fleeting thoughts about being accepted by other people, or even the natural disposition to incline toward such acceptance, al-Ghazali does not consider repelling them to be within the realm of human responsibility, perhaps because, in and of themselves, such thoughts and inclinations do not necessarily directly lead to actions with ostentatious intentions.

Does the Attack of the Occurrence of Ostentation Harm You?[150]

Perhaps you might say that "I have decided all of this[151] in my heart, and my heart has shunned ostentation, but perhaps the occurrence of ostentation might attack me by surprise in an act of worship when someone happens to notice it. What is the cure for this attack?"

Know that the root of this cure is that you hide your acts of worship as you hide your evil deeds, and in this there is safety....

Its cure is that you renew in your heart that which was formerly firmly entrenched in it of the knowledge of being subjected to Allah's despising[152]—Mighty and Majestic is He—along with the incapacity of the people to help you or harm you, until there arises from it [the heart] the abhorrence of the cause of ostentation....[153]

154 That is, you may intend that your act of worship serve as an instructive example for an onlooker, as long as you don't additionally desire that people view you as pious.

155 Al-Fudayl ibn 'Iyad (d. 803 CE) was a dangerous highway bandit who repented rather suddenly upon hearing a verse of the Qur'an recited while trying to sneak into a house to see a slave girl with whom he had fallen in love. He changed his ways and lived out the rest of his life in Mecca, becoming a great ascetic worshipper. See al-Qushayri, *Al-Qushayri's Epistle on Sufism*, trans. Alexander D. Knysh, reviewed by Muhammad S. Eissa (Reading, UK: Garnet Publishing, 2007).

156 In matters where others might be affected by your actions, if you sense that you incline toward capricious motives, then you must turn away and escape. Out of scrupulousness, it was not uncommon for some of the pious early Muslims to flee from official positions, such as being appointed judge, out of fear of ostentation.

157 If a person is only praying in order to be praised and seen by others, such that there is no intention of worship, then it is not valid. A person should stop this action, for it is not considered prayer.

It Is Permissible to Make Known Your Acts of Obedience for the Sake of Emulation

It is permissible to make your acts of obedience known for the sake of emulation by the people and in order to awaken in them a desire [for such acts], as long as your intention is sound and it is not accompanied by a hidden desire....[154]

Likewise, it is permissible to conceal your disobedience and sins, but with the condition that your aim is not that people will believe you to be religiously scrupulous.... It is fine if the veiling of your disobedience gladdens you, and its manifestation saddens you. [It is fine] if you are happy with Allah's veiling it, or with [its veiling] being in conformity to Allah's command (for indeed Allah Most High loves the concealing of disobedience and forbids making it known). [Likewise, it is fine] if [your sadness] is because you dislike being censured since it pains you (and the pain of the people's censuring is not forbidden, rather it is necessarily natural). Moreover, that which is forbidden is being gladdened by the praise of the people for your acts of worship....

As for leaving acts of obedience out of fear of ostentation, there is no basis for it. Al-Fudayl[155] said, "Ostentation is leaving an action out of fear of ostentation." As for action for the sake of the people, it is polytheism. Rather, you must act while also doing so with sincerity, except for when the action is connected to the people, such as giving a legal verdict, leading the people [e.g., in governance], or sermonizing.[156]

As for the ritual prayer and charity, you should not leave them except when there is absolutely no intention for worship present therein. Rather, if the intention for ostentation is removed, then a person's action is not valid, so let him leave it.[157] As for the person who has become accustomed to doing a given action, and then a group arrives, and he fears ostentation for himself, it is not necessary that he leave the action, rather it is necessary that he persevere and continue his act of worship, and strive to repel the occurrence of ostentation and its causes.

158 A sound heart is one in which all the diseases are absent, not just some of them.

159 Both Abu Dawud and al-Tirmidhi narrate this in their collections with a high level of surety that it is attributed to the Prophet. In the language of the hadith scholars, it has a sound chain of narration (*hasan sahih*).

160 The outward form is usually not considered beautiful unless its entirety is beautiful. Likewise, the inward form is not fully beautiful if there remains something of the blameworthy traits. If you have the wisdom to know right from wrong, truth from falsehood, good action from bad action, you possess what al-Ghazali calls the "head of virtues." When you submit your anger and desire to the indications of wisdom and the sacred law's commands, then anger and desire serve you like a dog and a horse serve the hunter. From the harmonizing of a few core traits, the rest of the meritorious traits follow and good character arises. Al-Ghazali hints at it here, but goes in to greater detail in *The Revival of the Religious Sciences*.

☐ The Entirety of [Blameworthy] Character Traits and the Places Where You Fall into Delusions with Regard to Them

Know that blameworthy character traits are many, but their foundations all go back to what we have mentioned above. It is not sufficient that you purify the self of some traits, until it is purified of all [blameworthy traits]. Even if you were to leave just one of them predominant in you, that would call you back to the others, because they are bound up with each other, while one entails the other. No one is saved except the one who comes to Allah with a sound heart.[158]

The Prophet said, "The heaviest of that which is placed on the scale is good character."[159]

Much has been said regarding the reality of character and its definition. Most of what has been said treats some of its fruits and does not encompass all of the details. That which will apprise you of its reality is that you know that the created things and character are two expressions, and the intent of created things is the outward form, while character refers to the inward form. That is because the human being is composed of a body, which is perceived with eyesight, and a soul and self that are perceived with the spiritual insight, not eyesight. For each one of them is a form, whether it is ugly or beautiful.[160]

(continued on page 207)

161 Just as there are gradations between ugly and beautiful, so too are there degrees of character between bad character and good character. You do not need to achieve total goodness in order to be saved; rather, your happiness in the next life will likely be in relation to the degree of good character you have achieved within the spectrum of bad and good character.

162 At its root, *mujahadah* refers to striving to break the habits of the self and getting it accustomed to resisting its passions and base inclinations.

163 As mentioned earlier, *riyadah* (translated here as "spiritual exercise") has been defined in several ways. It generally refers to living an austere life, disciplining your self through limiting your carnal desires (e.g., food, drink, sleep) to what facilitates and promotes remembrance of Allah and other praiseworthy actions and spiritual states.

164 Seek someone honest, pious, and of good character to judge you. In this case, you may need to make the person aware of some of your faults, because sometimes these may be hidden or connected to other things. Likewise, there may be some doubtful matters, such as thinking that you are getting angry for the sake of Allah, but really it is for your own ego; or thinking that you have performed a good deed so that it will be emulated, but really you sought to be raised in rank in the eyes of others. Just as entrusting your body or mind to a doctor or therapist is built on faith in his or her qualifications, likewise, in matters of character, you should not entrust your spiritual well-being to just anyone. Therefore, some scholars have listed qualifications for a Sufi *shaykh*. See Nuh Ha Mim Keller, *A Sea without Shore* (Beltsville, MD: Amana Publications, 2011).

165 Life is short. Spending it chasing after wealth and worldly things is nonsense, because the world is finite, while the afterlife is eternal. The Lord of the *dunya* and the Lord of the afterlife is one and the same, as al-Ghazali reminds us; thus, whatever you attain in this life is from Allah, but the afterlife is "better and more lasting."

The Path of Rectifying Your Character[161] Is Striving and Spiritual Exercise

The path of rectifying all of these character traits is striving[162] and spiritual exercise....[163]

And You Thought You Had Good Character!

Know that you supposed you had good character, while you were devoid of it. Take care not to be deluded. It is necessary that you appoint someone to judge you in this matter, other than yourself, and ask of him that he does not flatter you, but judges you honestly and insightfully....[164]

Examine the Blameworthy Character Traits in Your Heart

It is necessary that you examine these blameworthy and ruinous traits in your heart, and begin in order of importance, and turn toward the most predominant of these attributes, and break them gradually by degree.

I think that the most predominant blameworthy trait in you is love of the world, and the rest of the bad actions and character traits follow it. It is not possible for you to be rescued from the *dunya* except that you seek an empty cloister, in which you contemplate your turning to the *dunya* and turning away from the afterlife. You will not find a cause for this other than pure ignorance and heedlessness....[165]

166 To leave the *dunya* does not mean to leave this world in the sense of death, but rather to let go of it and leave your attachment and involvement with worldly matters.

167 If you have certainty in a cash payment, but doubts about the reality of a delayed payment, you will want to play it safe by taking the cash now.

168 Al-Ghazali divides them thus, in a passage omitted from the translation and summarized below:

1. Those who affirm heaven and hell as narrated in the Qur'an, having heard of heaven's various joys and the hardships of hellfire.

2. Those who do not affirm the sensory pleasure or pain of the afterlife; rather, they affirm them by way of ideational conception, like in a dream....

3. Those who affirm mental pain and delight and claim that they are greater than sensory pain and suffering.

These three aforementioned categories are those who reflect on divine matters. They include the prophets and saints, as well as the philosophers. All of them agree on affirming eternal happiness and eternal misery (however, they disagree over what form this will take). Indeed, you do not attain happiness except by leaving the *dunya* and turning toward Allah Mighty and Majestic....

4. The fourth category are not from among those who reflect on divine matters; rather, they include the natural philosophers (*atba'*) and the astrologers, who limit their reflection to the four humors and temperaments.

The atheists, too—if they possess even a little intelligence—may leave the *dunya* because of its many distresses, the speed with which it vanishes, and the vileness of its participants.

If Only You Were from the Masters of Spiritual Insights

Perhaps you might say, "The consequences of the matters of the *dunya* have been revealed to me manifestly before my eyes, and my heart has certainty in it. As for the matter of the afterlife, I have not witnessed it, and I do not find true affirmation in my heart. With that, I become tepid in my desire to leave the *dunya*[166]—which is like cash in hand—for that which is promised on credit, and upon which I cannot depend."[167]

I would say: If only you were from the masters of spiritual insights, then the matter of the afterlife would be disclosed to you as clearly as the matter of the *dunya* has been disclosed to you. If you are not from its people [i.e., the people of spiritual insights], then you should contemplate what the masters of spiritual insight have said, for the people with regard to the afterlife are of four categories....[168]

So if you are not one who has an opinion about the afterlife, and you do not witness the tribulations of the *dunya* with certainty, then you are foolish and misled, so you shall certainly know its tidings after a while. With that, Allah Most High says in the Qur'an, "Leave them alone, to enjoy (the good things of this life) and to please themselves; let (false) hope amuse them; soon will knowledge (undeceive them)" [15:3].

BOOK IV
Meritorious
Character Traits

◈ In his introduction to Book IV, al-Ghazali says, "The meritorious character traits which you seek to adorn yourself are also ten." Your spiritual path is not completed by merely ridding yourself of ruinous and blameworthy traits. Rather, you must also adorn yourself with the meritorious traits commanded in the Qur'an and hadiths of the Prophet Muhammad. It is fitting that the first of these meritorious traits is repentance (*tawbah*), as you admit thereby your imperfection, because no one is ever totally rid of sin and bad character, save the prophets.

1 This hadith has been narrated by Ibn Majah with this wording. Al-Ghazali cites it with the following additional sentence preceding it: "The one who repents is beloved to Allah."

2 Belief is the starting point of repentance, it being knowledge of the ruinous nature of the transgression. Regarding a past sin, you must be remorseful and do your utmost to remedy the effects of it, such as returning stolen goods, apologizing to someone who has been wronged, and so on. At any given moment, your responsibility is to leave a bad action immediately, if you have already fallen into it. Regarding the future, you must be resolved to never again commit the bad action. With that, you obtain complete repentance.

3 Turning to Allah in repentance is an obligation because it entails knowing the ruinous and prohibited actions and the necessity of leaving them. Knowledge of the commands and prohibitions that are unequivocally mentioned in the Qur'an and on the tongue of the Prophet is a part of faith. In this verse of the Qur'an, success or bliss in the afterlife is linked to repentance.

THE FIRST FOUNDATION

☐ Repentance

Verily, it is the beginning of the path for the spiritual traveler, and the key to felicity.

Allah Most High says, "... For Allah loves those who turn to Him constantly and He loves those who keep themselves pure and clean" [2:222].

Allah also says, "... And O ye believers! Turn ye all together toward Allah, that ye may attain bliss" [24:31].

The Prophet said, "The one who repents from sin is like one who has no sins."[1]

The Reality of Repentance

The reality of repentance is returning to Allah Most High from the path of being distant to the path of nearness. However, there is a necessary pillar of repentance, a starting point for it, and a complete perfection of repentance....[2]

Repentance Is an Obligation for All

If you know the reality of repentance, it is clear to you that it is an obligation for all, in every state.

Allah Most High says, "... And O ye believers! turn ye all together toward Allah, that ye may attain bliss" [24:31].

In the above verse, Allah is addressing absolutely everyone.[3]

4   Indeed, for each state or level a person may reach, there is a flaw from which he must repent. After listing a number of states and the bad character traits of which those at that level must rid themselves, al-Ghazali closes with mention of the repentance of the person who knows Allah experientially.

5   That is to say that you can continually draw nearer to Allah, and since no human being is without flaw, there is always something from which to repent.

6   With each good deed, the heart is purified, and with each bad deed, it is darkened. Al-Tirmidhi narrates from the Prophet with what the hadith scholars call a sound (authentic) chain of transmission, "Follow up a bad deed with a good one, as it will wipe it out." While this hadith can be interpreted as referring to erasing a bad deed from your account in the afterlife, al-Ghazali opines that repentance's effects are also perceivable in this life, that is, through the purification of the heart and readying it for the experience of gnosis. When Allah accepts your repentance, the heart is ready to accept the lights of gnosis.

7   First, the person who has a sickness of the heart is not aware of his illness. Second, the consequences of this sickness are not made apparent to him in this world, as the death of the heart is not apparent in the way that the death of the body by way of physical illness is. Third, al-Ghazali says that in his day and age—and certainly in ours as well— the physicians themselves are so ridden with the diseases of the heart that they fail to properly administer treatment. For more details, see M. S. Stern's translation of the chapter on repentance from *The Revival of the Religious Sciences*, page 166ff. (www.Ghazali.org/books/gz-repent.pdf).

Humans Are Not Free of Sin

As for the obligation of repentance in every state, it is because the human being is not free from sin in all of his states, neither in his limbs nor in his heart. Nor is he free from those bad character traits of which he must necessarily purify himself, for indeed they distance him from Allah. Busying yourself with their removal is repentance, for it is returning from the path of being distant to the path of nearness.

If you are free of all that, you are not free from heedlessness of Allah, and that is also the path of being distant. It is necessary that you return from it by way of remembrance.

Allah Most High says, "... Call thy Lord to mind when thou forgettest" [18:24].... **4**

As for the repentance of those who know Allah experientially, it is repenting from stopping at a station that is considered to be behind the gnostic's station. The stations of nearness to Allah are endless, as is the repentance of the person who knows Allah experientially.**5**

The Acceptance of Repentance

If the conditions of repentance are present, then it is definitely accepted, and you need not be concerned over this so long as you understand that the meaning of "acceptance" is that your heart is prepared for the acceptance of the lights of gnosis to be manifested in it....**6**

The Remedy of Repentance

The remedy of repentance is achieved by way of untying the knot of persistence [in sin], for nothing prevents you from repentance except persistence, which is a sickness in the heart. Its cure is like the bodily cures, except this sickness is greater than the sickness of the body for three reasons.**7**

(continued on page 217)

8   The five matters are as follows:

1. The punishment for sins is delayed until after death, and thus not immediate.

2. Desires for the prohibited are strong, oppressive, and immediate.

3. Excessive hope that your pious deeds will wipe out your sins often causes the believer to delay repentance and persist in sin.

4. Knowledge that sins are forgivable and do not necessarily lead to punishment, because Allah might forgive you, causes a person to depend excessively on hope, without having the sufficient balance of fear.

5. The previous four causes relate to the believer. The fifth pertains to a person who doubts the prophets, which is a form of disbelief. The person who doubts the truthfulness of the prophets' claims thereby falls into prohibited actions, believing there to be no punishment for them.

Al-Ghazali mentions the main cure to these ailments to be contemplation (*fikr*). He explains the cures to contemplate for each of these causes in detail in *The Revival of the Religious Sciences*. See M. S. Stern's translation of the chapter on repentance from *Revival*, page 128ff. (www.Ghazali.org/books/gz-repent.pdf).

9   The major sins are in many cases those that infringe on the rights of Allah, such as worshipping another being, or those that infringe on the rights of a fellow human being, such murder, theft, abuse, and so on. These sins require repentance, with all of its conditions mentioned above. Lesser sins might include engaging in excessive amounts of vain conversation or failing to turn away from that which is prohibited to view. Lesser sins are said to be cleansed from a person's record with performing the requisite ablutions before prayer and by the prayer itself, as well as other acts of worship or piety. Persistence in these lesser sins, however, is counted as a major sin and thus requires repentance. Indeed, the repetition of smaller sins, al-Ghazali informs us, has a major role in darkening the heart, just as a steady flow of water droplets will bore through a stone.

Regarding the remedy of repentance [by way of breaking the persistence in sin] , you must look to the causes of persistence, which return to five matters....[8]

Repentance from All Sins Is an Obligation

Repentance from all sins is an important obligation, most importantly from the major sins. Persistence in minor sins is a major sin, so there is no minor sin if one persists in it. Likewise, there is no major sin with returning to Allah and seeking His forgiveness.[9]

10 Allah Himself is the object of our love, yet we fear His ability to punish and distance us. Allah is therefore not merely a being to be feared, whose mention causes only dread and concern, but rather love of Allah the Most Merciful is considered to be the most important human emotion with regard to Him. Yet love and hope must be balanced by fear to keep us on the straight path.

11 This hadith has been narrated by al-Bayhaqi. The authenticity of this hadith does not reach the level such that it can be claimed with reasonable surety that the Prophet said it; in the technical terminology of hadith scholars, its chain of narration is weak.

12 A person who finds himself in a lion's den does not fear it if he does not know what a lion is. However, whoever knows the nature of a lion, and its potential to destroy, necessarily fears it. Likewise, a person who knows Allah, His majesty, and His absolute independence, and also knows that He has created heaven and hell and their respective inhabitants, necessarily has *haybah* (awe, reverence, and fear), which al-Ghazali considers the most perfected type of fear.

THE SECOND FOUNDATION

☐ Fear

Allah has combined guidance, mercy, knowledge, and satisfaction for those who fear Him.**10**

Allah Most High says, "When the anger of Moses was appeased, he took up the tablets: in the writing thereon was guidance and mercy for such as fear their Lord" [7:154].

He Most High also says, "Those truly fear Allah, among His servants, who have knowledge; for Allah is exalted in might, oft-forgiving" [35:28].

Allah Most High also says, "Those who have faith and do righteous deeds, they are the best of creatures" [98:7].

The Prophet said, "The summit of wisdom is fear of Allah."**11**

The Reality of Fear of Allah Most High

Know that the reality of fear is the suffering and burning of the heart on account of the anticipation of something severely disliked in the future. Perhaps that fear stems from a flowing of sins, or perhaps the fear of Allah Most High stems from knowledge of His attributes that necessitate fear, and this is more complete. This is because a person who knows Allah fears Him by necessity.**12**

With that, Allah Most High says, "Those truly fear Allah, among His servants, who have knowledge; for Allah is exalted in might, oft-forgiving" [35:28].

13   That is, if you cannot witness those gnostics possessing spiritual states such as fear of Allah, you should endeavor to hear about them.

14   The foolishly heedless are like the child who doesn't look to his father and learn to be fearful of a serpent. Though his father knows with certainty by experience, the child remains ignorant unless he witnesses this fear from his father and adopts it.

The Remedy of Fear and Its Attainment

The remedy of fear and its explanation is according to two ranks:

1. The first is knowledge of Allah Most High; indeed, it necessitates fear. Indeed, a person who falls into a lion's claws is not in need of a treatment in order to fear it if he knows what a lion is. Whomever knows the Majesty of Allah Most High, His Independence, and that He created heaven and its folk, and that He created hell and its folk, and that His word has been fulfilled in truth and in justice regarding felicity and distress with respect to every person, and that it is inconceivable that this be changed, and that nothing can divert Him from executing His Pre-eternal Decree, and that the servant does not know what Allah's decree has previously established for him, and that he does not know what end he will be given to meet, and that he deems it possible that he be destined to everlasting distress, for such a person [who knows the above], it is not conceivable that he not fear [Allah].

2. As for one who is unable [to know] the reality of gnosis, then his treatment is to look at those who are fearful, and to witness their states, or to hear about that.[13] Indeed, the prophets are the most fearful among Allah's creation, along with the saints, the scholars, and the people of spiritual insight. Those among Allah's creation who feel the safest [from Allah's decree] are the foolishly heedless whose view does not extend to what has come before nor what is to be the end, nor to knowing the Majesty of Allah Most High. This is like the child who does not fear a serpent unless he witnesses his father fearful and fleeing from it, while his horse trembles when it sees it. The child witnesses this and follows his father, perceiving his fear, even if he does not know with certain knowledge the characteristic of the serpent....[14]

(continued on page 223)

15 If your fear is to such an extent that you turn to despair, forgetting
Allah's mercy, then that is blameworthy and you must balance it with
sufficient hope. In general, your fear should predominate in order to
repel the inclinations toward sin; however, as one nears death, hope
must predominate, as having a good opinion of Allah must overtake
you. The Prophet said, as narrated in the hadith collections of Muslim
ibn Hajjaj, Ahmad ibn Hanbal, Abu Dawud, and Ibn Majah, "Not one
of you should die except that he has a good opinion of his Lord."
Hope (raja') is not mere wishful thinking, like a person who hopes for his
garden to grow without planting a seed or tending to it. Rather, hope
is for the person who takes whatever means are available and hopes
that Allah keeps harm from his garden and that a harvest is possible
after the garden begins to bloom.

16 Fearful thoughts that do not result in action are not manifestations
of true fear; rather, they are just thoughts with no effect. True fear, as
mentioned below, is what, at minimum, instigates action, such as doing
what is commanded and avoiding what is prohibited, and manifests in
abstaining from worldly attachments.

We have narrated the states of the fearful in the chapter on fear in *The Revival of the Religious Sciences*. So let the one who is incapable of the apex of knowledge look attentively to the states of the prophets, saints, and gnostics, in order to know the truest among them in fear. If he truly contemplates that, his fear will overtake him.

Fear Is a Whip That Drives the Servant to Felicity

Fear is a whip that drives the servant to felicity. However, it must not be excessive such that it causes despair, as that is blameworthy. Rather, if fear gets the better of a person, it is necessary that he mixes hope with it....[15]

The fruit of hope is awakening the desire for seeking, and the fruit of fear is awakening the desire for fleeing, for whoever hopes for something seeks it, and whoever fears something flees from it. The lowest degree of fear is that which induces you to leave sins and to turn away from the *dunya* [world], and that which does not induce you to that is the mere chatter of the self.[16] Thoughts have no weight ... and there is no benefit in them; rather, fear, if it is complete, results in abstinence in the *dunya*, so we shall now mention abstinence and its meaning.

17   Known in the Hebrew Bible as Korah, one of the followers of Moses, he is known in the Qur'an as Qarun. His story is an example of haughtiness, excessive wealth, and greed. See Numbers 16 in the Hebrew Bible for the biblical narrative. *Surah* 28:76–80 has the Qur'anic narrative.

18   This hadith has been narrated by Ibn Majah and deemed sound by Imam al-Nawawi. Yahya ibn Sharaf al-Nawawi, popularly known as Imam Nawawi, was a thirteenth-century scholar of law, hadith, and Sufism, who was deeply impacted by al-Ghazali's legal and mystical teachings.

 Abstinence

Allah Most High says, "Nor strain thine eyes in longing for the things We have given for enjoyment to parties of them, the splendor of the life of this world, through which We test them; but the provision of thy Lord is better and more enduring" [20:131].

He Most High also says, "To any that desires the tilth of the hereafter, We give increase in his tilth, and to any that desires the tilth of this world, We grant somewhat thereof, but he has no share or lot in the hereafter" [42:20].

Allah Most High says with regard to Qarun:[17] "So he went forth among his people in the (pride of his worldly) glitter. Said those whose aim is the life of this world, 'Oh! that we had the like of what Qarun has got! For he is truly a lord of mighty good fortune!' But those who had been granted (true) knowledge said, 'Alas for you! The reward of Allah (in the hereafter) is best for those who believe and work righteousness; but this none shall attain, save those who steadfastly persevere (in good)'" [28:79–80].

Allah makes clear that abstinence is from the fruits of knowledge.

The Prophet said, "Be abstinent with regard to the *dunya* and Allah will love you; be abstinent of what is in the hands of the people and they will love you."[18]

19   Implicit in this is that your home, clothes, food, and furnishings are not excessive, merely what suffices. There are levels to abstinence in these matters, such as a person whose home is a corner in a mosque, whose food is enough to avoid hunger in that moment, whose clothes are enough to just cover what is mandated by the sacred law, and whose furnishings are a comb and a clay jug.

The Reality of Abstinence with Regard to the World

Abstinence with regard to the world has a reality, a root, and a fruit.

As for its reality, it is aversion of the self from the *dunya* and withdrawing from it in obedience according to your ability.

As for its root, it is knowledge and light that shines in the heart until the breast is expanded and gladdened by it. By this root, it is made clear that the next life is better and more lasting, and that this world in relation to the next world is less than a piece of clay compared to a gem.

As for its fruit, it is contentment with the *dunya* to the extent of what is necessary, namely, the provisions of a rider. The root is the light of gnosis, which produces the state of withdrawing (from the *dunya*), while the limbs become capable of refraining from all except the necessary provisions of travel. The necessities of the provisions of travel are a place to live, clothes, food, and furnishings.[19]

The Degrees of Abstinence

Abstinence is of several degrees:

1. The first is that a person is abstinent, but his self inclines toward the *dunya*, though he struggles against his self. Such a person is attempting abstinence, but he is not one who is abstinent. However, this is the beginning of abstinence.

2. The second is that a person's self has an aversion to the world and does not incline toward it, due to his knowledge that it is not possible to join between the world and blessings of the next world. Such a person permits his self to leave its attachment to the world, like the self of one who freely spends a dirham in order to purchase a precious gem; if the dirham was beloved to him, then this is abstinence.

(continued on page 229)

20 Your abstinence should not be like a person who is kept away from the king's palace by vicious guard dogs, who, if the dogs were not there, would happily enter the palace and enjoy its luxuries. Rather, the perfected abstinence is that your heart is empty of attachment to that from which you abstain. As one Sufi put it, abstinence is not that your hand is empty, but rather that your heart is empty of what is in your hands.

3. The third is that a person's self is not inclined toward the world, nor is it averse to it; rather, the world's existence or nonexistence is tantamount to the same thing. Financial wealth with such a person would be like water, and Allah's treasure would be like an ocean to him.... This is the most perfect form of abstinence.

The Perfection of Abstinence

The perfection of abstinence is abstinence with regard to abstinence....[20]

The Degrees of Those Who Aspire to Abstinence

Those who aspire to abstinence are of three degrees:

1. The first is that the person aspiring to it is afraid of the fire of hell. This is the abstinence of the fearful ones.

2. The second is higher than the previous, and it is that the person aspiring to it desires the blessings of paradise. This is the abstinence of the hopeful. Worship inspired by hope is better than worship inspired by fear, because hope requires love.

3. The third, and it is the highest, is that the person who aspires to abstinence is contemptuous of inclining toward that which is other than Truth, keeping the self from it, and despising what is other than Allah.

21 A person who has been restrained from the pleasures of the *dunya* because of poverty, despite his heart's attachment to that which he lacks, is still of a higher degree than a wealthy person who immerses himself in worldly pleasures until he finds comfort in them. The sorrow of a rich and worldly person at death is likely more extreme because he is leaving a false paradise and quite probably not headed toward the true paradise. To the poor person whose heart is attached to the *dunya*, it is as though he is leaving a prison and quite possibly headed toward paradise, having been protected from the evils of the *dunya*, except in the case of the person who failed the test of poverty and fell into greater sins.

The Degrees of Those Things from Which You Abstain

Abstinence with regard to those things from which you abstain is of a number of degrees. Its perfection is abstinence from all other than Allah Most High in this life and the next. Beneath that degree is abstinence with regard to the world in particular, but not the afterlife. Then there enters into it all in which there exists prosperity and enjoyment in the *dunya*, from wealth, prestige, and luxury. Beneath that is that you abstain from wealth but not prestige or from some things to the exclusion of others. That is a weak form of abstinence, because prestige is sweeter and more desirable than wealth. Indeed, abstaining from prestige is more important.

Abstinence Is That You Withdraw from the World Out of Obedience

Abstinence is that you withdraw from the world out of obedience while having the ability to engage in it. As for the world being withdrawn from you while you desire it, that is poverty, not abstinence....**21**

Know that a person who is poor yet content with whatever has been given to him, without being covetous of seeking [the *dunya*], his rank is near to the one who is abstinent....

In short, the reward of the poor person becomes great when he is content and patient. A poor person's being pleased with Allah and what He has given him and having patience are the foundation of abstinence. These stations are not complete without patience, so we shall now mention it.

22 Allah combines both blessings and mercy for the patient, something not mentioned in combination for others than those who are patient.

23 This hadith has been narrated in numerous collections and deemed sound by many scholars.

24 When you experience the inclination to do a bad action, the reality of patience as intended here is that you counter the allure of evil with the commitment to follow the commands of the sacred law, rather than give in to it. In a sense, one might say it is patient perseverance in doing good deeds, despite the onslaught of evil inclinations.

25 Human beings experience both the incitement toward vain desires as well as the incitement toward desiring to experience beauty of the Divine Presence. The former incitements are typically from what al-Ghazali calls the "armies of the devil," addressing themselves to vain desires, while the latter are from the "party of Allah and His angels," who address themselves to the intellect.

THE FOURTH FOUNDATION

☐ Patience

Allah Most High says in the Qur'an, "And obey Allah and His Messenger, and fall into no disputes, lest ye lose heart and your power depart; and be patient and persevering. For Allah is with those who patiently persevere" [8:46].

And He combined matters for those who are patient that were not combined for others,[22] saying, "They are those on whom (descend) blessings from Allah, and mercy, and they are the ones that receive guidance" [2:157]....

Allah Glorified is He mentions patience in the Qur'an in excess of seventy places.

The Prophet said, "Patience is half of faith."[23]

The Reality of Patience

The reality of patience is establishing the incitement to religion when encountering the incitement to vain desire.[24] Patience (in this sense) is unique to the human condition in that humans are a composite of both angelic and bestial races....[25]

26   A person who has given in to his vain desires and has lost hope in ever turning away from them is destroyed, because he has forgotten that there is always an opportunity for repentance. The doors to repentance are open until just before the soul departs from a dying person. Hope and fear are obligatory, and success is found in the balance.

27   Such a person's intellect has become the prisoner of his vain desires, according to al-Ghazali.

28   The battle between the call to vain desire and the call to religious piety wages on for such a person, and each side wins some and loses some.

29   This battle against vain desires is what al-Ghazali and others refer to as *jihad al-akbar*, "the greatest struggle," in comparison to actual defensive martial battles, which are considered the lesser struggle.

The Degrees of Patience

Patience has three degrees with regard to weakness and strength:

The highest rank is that the call of vain desire is entirely suppressed, such that there remains no power for it to resist. You attain to it by enduring patience and protracted spiritual struggle. That is from those of whom it is said, "Verily those who say, 'Our Lord is Allah,' and remain firm (on that Path), on them shall be no fear, nor shall they grieve" [46:13].

The lowest rank is that you are incapable of repelling the call to vain desires and you drop the struggle for incitement to religion. Vain desires gain ascendency, and the heart submits to the army of Satan. That is from those of whom it is said, "If We had so willed, We could certainly have brought every soul its true guidance; but the Word from Me will come true, 'I will fill hell with jinns and men all together'" [32:13].

The signs of a person with the lowest level of patience are two:

1. The first is that he says, "I yearn for repentance, but it is difficult for me, and I do not hope for it." Such is one who is despondent, and the despondent are doomed....[26]

2. The second is that there does not remain in him the desire for repentance, but he says, "Allah is generous and merciful, and He is in no need of my repentance."[27] ... We seek refuge in Allah from such a person.

The middle rank is that there is no abatement in the battle; however, the war between them is alternating in success....[28] The sign of this is that you leave those vain desires that are weakest, and you are unable to leave that which is in the majority.[29]

30   Such a person does not think of being patient, because he indulges himself in all that he desires, forgetting his ultimate beginnings and where he will end up.

31   As mentioned briefly earlier, the term *jihad* means "struggle." There is the struggle against the lower self (*nafs*), which is the primary struggle, and there is also the struggle against a hostile aggressor. Regarding the latter, many scholars, if not most, have argued that war is permissible only in defense of one's self, people, land, and religion or in defense of the oppressed. Others believe in an offensive war, but in the context of a world in which nations are at war by default, wherein the state of war can only be lifted by an explicit peace treaty. Such a worldview indicates that an "offensive war" in this context is a preemptive strike against an already established hostile enemy. Because we live in a world today in which the opposite is true—that is, the default state is presumed to be peace—in the absence of an open declaration of war it is difficult to apply this less popular opinion. In any case, despite the justifications for going to war, the ethics of warfare demand a very wide conception of noncombatant and a very narrow definition of combatant. Noncombatant immunity is the prophetic teaching and the mainstream understanding of Islam. Terrorism, that is, politically motivated attacks against civilians in order to strike fear into the noncombatant citizens of an enemy's nation, is antithetical to the traditional Islamic ethos, that is, totally un-Islamic.

The General Need for Patience

Know that the need for patience is a general need in all states, because the entirety of what a person encounters in this life is not devoid of two things, namely, that you assent to your vain desires or you oppose them:

1. If a person assents to his vain desires, such as health and well-being, richness and rank, having a lot of kinfolk, then he does not need patience with them....[30]

2. That which opposes vain desires is of four types:

    a. Acts of obedience: The self shies away from some of them due to laziness, such as the ritual prayer, and shies away from others due to stinginess, such as the poor tax, and still from others due to both, such as the pilgrimage and defensive struggle against an aggressor.[31] Patience in obedience is among the most difficult things.

        The obedient person is in need of patience in three states:

        i.   At the beginning of an act of worship, by making sound his sincerity. Patience is also required in repelling the bad traits of ostentation and the machinations of the devil, the self, and their deceptions.

        ii. At the time of the act of worship, in order not to lazily neglect the fulfillment of its obligatory components and superogatory components. That is only possible on condition that you have etiquette with the presence of the heart and negating neurotic misgivings.

        iii. After the conclusion [of the act of worship], by patiently refraining from mentioning the act of worship and from disclosing it in order to manifest ostentation and a good reputation. All of this sort of patience is harsh on the self.

(continued on page 239)

32   *Mujahid*, "striver," is the term often used for a person who fights off an aggressor in a just war, yet here, and elsewhere, the greater struggle (*jihad*) is against your base desires and ego.

33   The first part of this hadith is narrated, with slightly different wording, by al-Tirmidhi, while the second half is narrated by Ibn Majah.

34   A prime example of such sins are those of the tongue, which are widespread and very difficult to avoid. These include backbiting (*ghibah*), talebearing (*namimah*), lying (*kadhb*), and so on. Al-Ghazali refers to the type of patience necessary to repel these as being from the harshest types of patience.

35   This has been narrated by al-Bayhaqi and other hadith collectors with some weakness in its transmission, though its meaning is in line with Islamic principles.

b. Acts of disobedience: The Prophet said, "The striver[32] is one who struggles against his vain desires, and the emigrant is one who emigrates from evil."[33] Patiently refraining from sins is the harshest, especially when refraining from a sin that has become habitual and customary.[34]

c. That which is not connected to the choice of the person, but, rather, he has a choice with regard to repelling it or being on guard against it, such as verbal or physical harm from another. Patience in this case is by leaving retribution, which at times is mandatory and at others highly recommended....

3. That over which the person has no choice at any point, such as the death of a loved one, the destruction of his wealth, sickness, losing a limb, and other types of tribulations. Patience with regard to these matters is from the highest stations....

You know that you are not free from having patience in all of your states, and by this it becomes clear that patience is a portion of faith. Its other portion is that which is connected to actions, namely thankfulness. The Prophet is reported to have said, "Faith is of two halves: one half is patience, the other half is thankfulness."[35] This is with regard to considering actions and designating them by faith.

36 The late-night prayers (*tahajjud*) are considered a strong recommendation for others, though not an obligation according to most. However, the Prophet used to pray them regularly. They are a means of drawing nearer to Allah and seeking forgiveness.

37 The "sins" of the prophets, who are divinely protected from going against the command of Allah, are not actual disobedience to Allah. Rather, they are the act of choosing one action that is of less merit than another.

38 This has been narrated in the hadith collection of Muslim ibn Hajjaj.

THE FIFTH FOUNDATION

□ Gratitude

Allah Most High says in the Qur'an, "They worked for him as he desired, (making) arches, images, basins as large as reservoirs, and (cooking) cauldrons fixed (in their places): 'Work ye, sons of David, with thanks! But few of My servants are grateful'" [34:13].

He Most High also says, "And remember! your Lord caused to be declared (publicly), 'If ye are grateful, I will add more (favors) unto you; but if ye show ingratitude, truly My punishment is terrible indeed'" [14:7].

He Most High also says, "Then do ye remember Me; I will remember you. Be grateful to Me, and reject not faith" [2:152].

"Muhammad is no more than an apostle, many were the apostles that passed away before him. If he died or were slain, will ye then turn back on your heels? If any did turn back on his heels, not the least harm will he do to Allah, but Allah (on the other hand) will swiftly reward those who (serve Him) with gratitude" [3:144].

"What can Allah gain by your punishment, if ye are grateful and ye believe? Nay, it is Allah that recognizeth (all good), and knoweth all things" [4:147].

The Prophet's wife Aisha reported that the Prophet would cry while performing his late-night prayers.**36** Aisha said, "Why do you cry, when Allah has forgiven you all of your**37** past and future sins?" The Prophet said, "Should I not be a thankful servant?"**38**

39   A lengthy discussion follows; it is summarized here: Knowledge is the root from which the spiritual state (*hal*) grows, and the spiritual state is that which produces action. These are three pillars of gratitude. The first pillar, that of knowledge, begins with knowledge of the blessing and the source of blessings, because you know that all blessings are from Allah Most High. This eventually leads to gnosis, the ultimate form of knowing. The second pillar, that of the spiritual state, is derived from gnosis, and it is gladness with Allah—the source of blessings—in the form of humility and reverence. The third pillar, that of action, is that you use the blessing you have received in good deeds, not in bad deeds; that is, when you are thankful for a blessing and realize its wisdom, you only use it for the sake of good and drawing nearer to Allah. The thankfulness of the eyes is to avert them from what is prohibited and to look upon the permissible. The thankfulness of the hands is to keep them from prohibited actions and to busy them with good deeds. The thankfulness of the ears is to keep them from listening to prohibited speech and the like and to let them hear the recitation of the Qur'an, permissible speech, and so on. When you know Allah is the source of blessing, reach gnosis, and are immersed in the contemplation and recognition of Allah's Oneness, Sanctity, Generosity, and other attributes, you are moved to action, including expressing gratitude, for which many rewards have been mentioned in various hadiths.

40   Al-Ghazali goes on to explain, by way of example, that if you look at a member of the opposite sex who is prohibited for you to look at, you have covered over or denied the many blessings of Allah found in the human eyes, the sun, and every blessing associated with sight. For you could not gaze were it not for having functional eyes and the light of the sun. Indeed, the eyes need sunlight, and the sun needs the sky, so it is as though you have denied all of the blessings found in the earth and the sky. Therefore, following the commands and prohibitions of Islamic law, as well as the demonstrative example of the Prophet, when contemplated in such a way, is the secret of achieving thankfulness.

Thankfulness Is among the Highest Spiritual Stations

Know that thankfulness is among the highest spiritual stations, even higher than patience, fear, abstinence, and the rest of the stations that have been previously mentioned. This is the case because they are not sought in and of themselves, rather they aim at other than themselves. What is sought from patience is vanquishing vain desires, while fear is a whip that drives on the fearful one toward the desired praiseworthy spiritual stations. Abstinence is to flee from attachments that busy one from Allah Most High. As for thankfulness, it is sought in and of itself. With that, it does not cease in heaven, whereas repentance, fear, patience, and abstinence are not found there.

Allah Most High says, "(This will be) their cry therein: 'Glory to Thee, O Allah.' And 'Peace' will be their greeting therein! And the close of their cry will be 'Praise be to Allah, the Cherisher and Sustainer of the worlds!'" [10:10].

You know that by knowing the reality of gratitude, and that it is composed of knowledge, state, and action....**39**

Who Is Capable of the Complete Perfection of Thankfulness?

Know that only he whose heart Allah has opened to the acceptance of submission [Islam] is capable of the complete perfection of thankfulness, for such a person is illuminated by a light from his Lord. He sees in everything its wisdom, its secret, and what is beloved to Allah in it. For the person who has not had that disclosed to him, he must follow the example of the Prophet and the rules of the sacred law, for therein are to be found the secrets of thankfulness....**40** Indeed, there is not a law from the laws of Allah except that there are found therein a spiritual secret, a special property, and wisdom.

The completion of thankfulness cannot be conceived except from a person who is totally sincere, so we shall now mention sincerity and truthfulness.

41 That is, seeking Allah Himself.

42 This hadith has been narrated by both al-Bukhari and Muslim ibn Hajjaj.

43 It is the will or desire that motivates you to action, and it arises from knowledge. The connection among knowledge, will, and action is discussed in the following sentences.

44 For example, if you are hungry, but your hunger is dormant, and your eyes fall upon some food, your hunger is awoken by the knowledge of the presence of food, and your hand reaches out, on account of this knowledge, to grab the food. Thus the action has been motivated by the will or desire, which in turn is sparked by the knowledge of the presence of food.

45 A sincere intention is one wherein the motivation itself is pure. If a man decides to give half of his wealth in charity so that he will become better known in the community, and perhaps thereby move up the social and professional ladder, while the action itself is noble, the intention is flawed, because it is motivated by love of wealth and status.

THE SIXTH FOUNDATION

☐ Sincerity and Truthfulness

Know that for sincerity there is a reality, a root, and complete perfection, and these three are necessary pillars. The root of sincerity is the intention when it is sincere. Its reality is negating defects from the intention. Its complete perfection is truthfulness.

The First Pillar: Intention

Allah Most High says in the Qur'an, "Send not away those who call on their Lord morning and evening, seeking His face ..." [6:52].

The meaning of intention is intending the countenance of Allah Most High.[41]

The Prophet said, "Verily actions are according to intentions...."[42]

The Reality of Intention

The reality of intention is the motivating desire for the power that originates from knowledge.[43] Its explanation is that the entirety of your actions are not sound except with power, will, and knowledge. Knowledge awakens will, and will evokes power, and power is the servant of will in that it moves the limbs....[44]

Intention, then, is the will that motivates, and the meaning of it being sincere is purifying the motivation from defects.[45]

(continued on page 247)

46   The actions of the heart, such as the remembrance of Allah, fear of Allah, and sincerely intending Allah's pleasure, are better than physical actions, because physical actions without the intention of seeking Allah's pleasure are just actions. Although some of them may have a positive outcome, such as feeding the poor, if your intention is that people will call you generous, then the action has lost its truest value, which is cutting the heart's attachment to wealth.

47   The Arabic term translated as "steadfastness" could imply being steadfast in performing acts of worship or staying in the mosque for a period of time as a sort of border guard, guarding the heartlands from an external attack.

48   It is from the Prophet's example (*sunnah*) to retreat to the mosque for the last ten days of the month of Ramadan, the month in which Muslims fast from before dawn until just after sunset. It is also possible to do throughout the year, whether overnight or even for just a few moments.

Intention Is One of Two Parts of Worship

If action is achieved by the motivation of the intention, then intention and acting according to it constitute the completion of worship. Indeed, intention is one of two parts of any act of worship. However, it is the better of the two parts because the actions of the limbs are not what are sought, except for their effect on the heart in order that it inclines toward good, shuns evil, and is free to contemplate and engage in remembrance that connects the heart to spiritual intimacy and knowledge, these two being the cause for one's felicity in the afterlife.... [46]

Strive to Multiply the Intention

If you know the merit of the intention and that it occupies and affects the goal on which your sights are set, then strive to multiply the intention in all of your actions, such that with one action you have multiple intentions. If you truly desire to be led to its path, then one example will suffice you, that is, that entering a mosque and sitting therein is an act of worship. It is possible that you intend thereby eight matters:

1. The first is that you believe that it is the house of Allah Mighty and Majestic, and that one who enters it visits Allah, therefore you intend that.

2. The second is the intention of steadfastness. [47]

3. The third is retreat, and its meaning is restraining your hearing, sight, and limbs from their customary movements; indeed, it is a part of fasting. [48]

4. The fourth is seclusion and repelling the distractions of daily life in order to cause your inner self to persist in contemplating the afterlife and how to prepare for it.

5. The fifth is being free to make remembrance of Allah and to listen to the remembrance of Allah or to allow others to hear it....

(continued on page 249)

49   That is, the mosque.

50   The phrase "brother in Allah" is a special degree of friendship between two people where they love each other for the sake of Allah and prefer each other over their own selves. Assisting and seeking to benefit such a brother has a great reward and treasure to be reaped in the afterlife. The mosque is the nesting place of such friendships, wherein friends meet and worship.

51   For all of your good deeds, you can contemplate multiple sound reasons for doing them. In intending all of these, rather than just one, you have increased the number of actions you have done, in a sense, and thereby increase the reward for them.

52   These are false intentions because they rely on causes that bring them into effect. They are not conceivably attainable without these causes, and thus such a thought that occurs to oneself is not properly an intention.

53   That is to say that a merely neutral action, such as buying a bottle of water, could become of a very high merit if the intention were something lofty, such as intending to give it to someone dying of thirst.

6. The sixth is to intend the teaching of sacred knowledge, and reminding one who forgets the ritual prayer, and forbidding the bad and commanding the good, such that you facilitate good things and shares in them.

7. The seventh is to abandon sins out of shyness toward Allah Mighty and Majestic, in that you confine yourself in His house[49] until you are embarrassed before Him that you would be tempted to commit a sin.

8. The eighth is that you benefit your "brother for the sake of Allah."[50]

So strive after this in the rest of actions, for by combining these intentions you purify and increase your actions....[51]

The Intention Is Not a Matter of Choice
Know that the intention is not a matter of choice. You should not be deceived such that you say with your tongue and heart, "I intend by sitting in the mosque this or that," and you suppose that you have intended, if you know beforehand that the intention is that which awakens and induces a person to action without which the existence of action is inconceivable.

The false intention is like the saying of a person "I intend to love so and so" or "I intend to be hungry" or "I intend to be satiated...."[52]

Whoever knows the reality of the intention, and knows that it is the soul of action, he does not follow his self to an action without a soul. Indeed, a neutral action could become more meritorious than an act of worship if an intention is present.[53]

Indeed, for the person who intends by eating and drinking the power to engage in acts of worship, and who does not have the intention of fasting at that time, then eating is better for him....

54   That is, an adulterated intention would entail that you intended both worship of Allah as well as something for your own self, such as being witnessed by others and called a righteous person.

55   The word al-Ghazali uses for "pure and unadulterated" is *khalisan*, which is derived from the same root as *ikhlas*. Thus "sincerity" has the additional implication of being free from other things that detract from its purity.

56   What is intended by this ostensibly strange statement is that if your actions are motivated by one purpose only, then you are technically sincere. If your sole purpose for praying in a congregation is so that people will call you pious, you have a singular motivation and intention, albeit faulty. Likewise, if your sole purpose for praying in a congregation is to earn Allah's pleasure and reward, then you have a singular motivation and intention. Customarily, however, the term "sincerity" is applied to a person with a singular motivation and intention that is considered lofty and appropriate.

57   Al-Ghazali mentions a number of examples of good actions that can be intended for the sake of Allah, but also mixed with other less noble, yet not impermissible intentions. In addition to the teacher of sacred knowledge who seeks both Allah's pleasure and obtaining a livelihood, he also mentions the person who fasts hoping to gain good health, the writer who seeks to improve his penmanship, the person who does his ritual ablutions in order to clean himself of things that are not impure (e.g., mud or food on his fingers), and so on. Although these additional intentions are not bad in and of themselves, they detract from the purity of an act of worship that should be done solely for the sake of Allah. Some scholars have said that the test of sincerity is that you would still do an action even if the additional permissible benefit (e.g., livelihood, improvement, health) were not present.

The Second Pillar: Sincerity of Intention

Allah Most High says in the Qur'an, "And they have been commanded no more than this: to worship Allah, offering Him sincere devotion, being true (in faith); to establish regular prayer; and to practice regular charity; and that is the religion right and straight" [98:5].

He Most High also says, "Is it not to Allah that sincere devotion is due?" [39:3].

He Most High also says, "Except for those who repent, mend (their lives), hold fast to Allah, and purify their religion as in Allah's sight; if so they will be (numbered) with the believers. And soon will Allah grant to the believers a reward of immense value" [4:146].

The Reality of Sincerity of Intention

The reality of sincerity is independence of the singular motivation. Its opposite is sharing, and it is that two motivations coexist.**54** If it is free from every impurity and flaw, it is called pure or unadulterated.**55**

You already know that the intention is incitement or motivation. A person who does not act except motivated by ostentation is sincere. A person who does not act except for Allah is sincere. However, the term is customarily applied specifically to one of the two....**56**

We have already mentioned that sincerity disappears with the presence of ostentation; however, it also vanishes if accompanied by other aims, such as a teacher who teaches sacred knowledge in order to seek a livelihood.**57**

If any of these additional aims have occurred in your actions, sincerity has already left, and this is a very weighty matter.

(continued on page 253)

58   If you still have sufficient intention to do something for the sake of Allah, then you are rewarded to the extent of that intention. As for whatever has been mixed with this intention, then there is no reward for it. Depending on the level of additional aims, your act of worship might be nullified, or at least your sincerity might be nullified. Al-Ghazali directs the reader to the more comprehensive chapter on ostentation in *The Revival of the Religious Sciences*.

59   This is quoted from a slightly longer statement found in an agreed-upon hadith of the Prophet recorded in Imam al-Nawawi's book *The Gardens of the Righteous* (Totowa, NJ: Rowman and Littlefield, 1975).

Flaws in Your Sincerity of Intention

Know that the mixing of these flaws is of multiple ranks; perhaps they predominate, or perhaps they overflow, or perhaps they are equal to the intention of worship and do not erase the root of reward in the neutral actions.[58]

The Third Pillar: Truthfulness

Allah Most High says in the Qur'an, "Among the Believers are men who have been true to their covenant with Allah. Of them some have completed their vow (to the extreme), and some (still) wait; but they have never changed (their determination) in the least" [33:23].

He Most High also says, "Also mention in the Book (the story of) Abraham; he was a man of Truth, a prophet" [19:41].

The Prophet said, "Indeed a man is truthful, and seeks the truth, until it is written with Allah that he is truthful." [59]

To know the merit of truthfulness, it suffices that you perceive the merit of the truthful. Know that there are six degrees of truthfulness; whoever achieves the degree of perfection in all of them is rightfully called "truthful":

1. The first is truthfulness in speech in all states, whether speaking about what is connected to the past, present, or future....

2. The second is truthfulness in intention. It is that you devote yourself completely to calling to the good....

3. The third is truthfulness in resolve. Indeed, sometimes a person resolves within himself that he would be truthful if he were to become wealthy, or that he would be honest if he were to attain a position of authority, but there might be weakness or a tendency to waiver in his resolve sometimes, while at other times he might have firm and unwavering conviction. Firm conviction is called truthful resolve.

(continued on page 255)

60 Such a person fulfills what he said he would do if such and such occurred. How many people enter politics, law, or business with the sincere intention of helping others, but fall short out of fear of losing wealth or stature or from being corrupted by their environment? It is one thing to talk the talk, but another to walk the walk.

61 This entails that your outer actions correspond with their inner states. If you stand in prayer with apparent humility, your mind should not be wandering in the affairs of the marketplace. Rather, inwardly, you must have the humility that your body indicates. Al-Ghazali narrates a hadith in this regard whose meaning is sound, but whose chain of transmission is weak: "The Prophet said, 'O Allah, make my inner secret greater than my external appearance, and make my external appearance virtuous.'"

62 The degrees of truthfulness in these matters are the highest, perhaps because these are considered the traits and states of the spiritual perfection of faith (*Ihsan*).

4. The fourth is truthfulness in fulfilling what you have resolved to do....[60]

5. The fifth is truthfulness in actions....[61]

6. The sixth is truthfulness in the stations of religion, and it is the highest of its gates. These include truthfulness in fear, hope, love, contentment, reliance, and others.[62]

These are the levels of truthfulness. Whoever is realized in all of them, then he is truthful. If some of these traits have not befallen a person, then his rank is according to the extent of his truthfulness. The totality of truthfulness entails the realization of the heart that Allah is the Sustainer and that reliance is upon Him, and thus we shall mention something of reliance upon Allah.

63   This hadith has been narrated in the collection of al-Tirmihi and al-Hakim—an eleventh-century hadith scholar from Nishapur—who declared it rigorously authenticated (*sahih*).

THE SEVENTH FOUNDATION

☐ Reliance on Allah

Allah Most High says in the Qur'an, "No reason have we why we should not put our trust on Allah. Indeed, He has guided us to the ways we (follow). We shall certainly bear with patience all the hurt you may cause us. For those who put their trust should put their trust on Allah" [14:12].

"... But on Allah put your trust if ye have faith" [5:23].

"Then, when thou hast taken a decision, put thy trust in Allah. For Allah loves those who put their trust (in Him)" [3:159].

"And if any one puts his trust in Allah, sufficient is Allah for him ..." [65:3].

The Prophet said, "If you thoroughly rely on Allah, He will provide your sustenance as He provides sustenance to birds who depart hungry and return satiated."[63]

64   The almond has an outer hull, beneath which is a hard shell that encases the nut. From the nut, almond oil is extracted. A person's monotheistic belief is akin to the almond; there is an outer shell, an inner shell, a core, and then an innermost core, as he goes on to explain.

65   Al-Ghazali does not think highly of a scholastic theologian whose only distinguishing characteristic from the common folk is the ability to repel heretical beliefs from true Islamic beliefs by way of rational proofs. Such a person is a believer but has not experienced the depths of faith if he does not move beyond this point of rational proofs into experiential faith.

66   Such a person, al-Ghazali tells us, sees the multiplicity of things in the universe and knows, through contemplation of the fact that every effect has a preceding cause, that all things of the universe ultimately originate from one doer. That is, he contemplates the cosmological proof for Allah's existence, which in its most basic form says that because every effect requires a preceding cause, then the universe had a beginning that was brought into being by a beginninglessly eternal ultimate cause (i.e., Allah), or it popped into existence without a cause, or it has existed eternally. He sees all the actions in the universe, their multiplicity, and their connectedness back to a primary doer, actor, or cause, for any other option (i.e., popping into existence without a cause or an infinite regress of causes and effects into the past) would be rationally absurd. Such a person is like the scholastic theologian, except that he has moved beyond debating and defending beliefs and has fully realized the truth of the arguments of the cosmological proofs, not just through rational affirmation, but through Allah's having opened his heart to it.

The Reality of Reliance

The reality of reliance means a state originating from affirming the Oneness of Allah. Its traces are manifest in actions.

There are three pillars of reliance, namely, gnosis, state, and action.

Spiritual knowledge is the root of reliance, by which I mean affirming the Oneness of Allah. It is relying on Allah without seeing any doer other than Him. The perfection of this spiritual knowledge is explained by your saying, "There is no God but Allah, the One with no partner, for Him is the dominion, for Him is the praise, and He has power over all things." For, within this statement is belief in the Oneness of Allah, and the perfection of power, generosity, and the wisdom that necessitates praise. Whoever says this truthfully with sincerity, his monotheism is complete, and the root is firmly established in his heart from which the state of reliance stems. I mean by "truthfully" that the meaning of the statement becomes a necessary attribute in his being, predominating over his heart, and leaving no room for the consideration of anything else.

This monotheistic belief has inner cores and outer layers, of which there are four levels. It is like the almond, which has a core, and the oil from it is the core of its core, and its outer shell is the shell of its shell.[64]

1. The outer shell is the statement of belief in monotheism with the tongue alone, and it is the faith of the hypocrite.

2. The inner shell is the belief in the heart with firm conviction, which is the belief of the common folk and scholastic theologians.[65]

3. The core is that the reality of this monotheistic belief has been disclosed to him by the light of Allah Mighty and Majestic.[66]

(continued on page 261)

67 Such a person sees the multiplicity in the universe as a matter of perspective. He realizes that all created things are ontologically connected to Allah's will, power, and knowledge and therefore have no real and independent existence in themselves. They are, rather, totally dependent on Allah's existence, will, power, and knowledge; thus, such a person fully realizes the meaning of "there is no power or might except with Allah." Nothing occurs in the universe except that it is willed by Allah, brought into being by His power, according to His knowledge. All created things are contingent and only merely possible, unlike Allah, who is the necessarily existent. This is *not* to be confused with pantheism, which sees that both Allah and the created universe are one.

68 Like the fourth category of monotheistic belief, or the innermost core of the almond metaphor, annihilation in the unity of Allah's entity (*fana'*) is the full recognition of Allah's ultimate power over everything. It is an experiential state described by many Sufis, though often with differing and confusing terms. It entails, according to al-Ghazali and those who follow him, an experience wherein a person does not witness anything of the created universe, not even himself, but rather, witnesses only Allah. This comes about from being enraptured in love and remembrance of Allah and is indeed quite rare. Al-Ghazali indicates that this high state is not necessary to reach the reality of reliance. Rather, you must know with certainty that everything you see among the multiplicity of created things originates from Allah's creative power.

69 Reliance on Allah will not be stirred up in you with the mere recognition of Allah being the sole source of all that occurs. Rather, this realization must be accompanied by the belief that every event occurs by way of Allah's mercy, generosity, and wisdom. There is no hardship or trial that is not accompanied by a greater underlying mercy and gift from Allah, be it spiritual, a reward in the afterlife, or something that leads to a greater good. Whatever occurs in the world, no matter how trivial or troublesome, occurs by Allah's wisdom.

4. The innermost core is that he does not see anything having existence except One or that he knows that there is only one existent.[67]

Reliance Necessitates Unity in Action

The reality of reliance is that it necessitates unity in action. It does not necessitate annihilation in the unity of Allah's entity.[68] Rather, the reliant one can see the multiplicity of created things, the means, and the causes; however, it is necessary that he witness the connection of their causal chain back to their originator.

How Do You Kindle the State of Reliance?

Faith in the unity of action and entity does not suffice in kindling the state of reliance, until belief in mercy, generosity, and wisdom are added to it.[69]

The second pillar of reliance is its spiritual state. Its meaning is that you put Allah Mighty and Majestic in charge of your affairs, that your heart relies on Him, that you are set at ease by entrusting yourself to Him, and that ultimately you do not heed any other than Him....

When your spiritual insight realizes that provision, appointing the time of death, creating, and commanding are under the control of Allah Most High and that He alone has control, without partner, and that His generosity, wisdom, and mercy are endless, and that His generosity and mercy are unparalleled by anyone, then your heart trusts and depends on Him necessarily, and you do not regard anything other than Him....

70   Among Allah's ninety-nine names are included *al-Wakeel* (the Trusted, Depended Upon, Trustee) and *al-Haqq* (the Real). Al-Ghazali mentions this perhaps to remind the reader that the words "reliance," "entrust" (*tawakkul*), and the Trusted (*al-Wakeel*) are all derived from the same root, *wa-ka-la*.

71   This is similar to granting someone the power of attorney to contract business or personal transactions on your behalf.

72   A child is mostly if not entirely oblivious to his reliance on his mother, because it is a natural state for him. Unlike the first level, that is, the one reliant on a lawyer or legal representative, this level of reliance is obtained through thought and reflection.

73   That is to say that you put up no resistance to the commands of the sacred law and are content with whatever befalls you. It has been described as annihilation of your will in Allah's will.

Levels of Reliance

If you know that reliance refers to a state of the heart with regard to trust in Allah the Trusted and True,[70] and with regard to abstaining from turning to other than Him, then know that there are three levels:

1. The first … is like the trust in the appointed representative in a legal dispute after you have belief in his perfection with regard to guidance, ability, and compassion.[71]

2. The second is stronger than the first, and it is similar to the state of a child with regard to his trust in his mother, and his fleeing to her in everything that afflicts him, and that is because of her compassion and protection. However, in his reliance, he is not aware of his reliance; indeed, he does not obtain it by thought and acquisition, even if his reliance was not free from a type of perception. As for reliance on the representative in a dispute [i.e., level one] it is like that which is obtained by thought and reflection.[72]

3. The third degree of reliance is the highest. It is that you are in the hands of Allah like the corpse is in the hands of the one who washes the dead.…[73]

(continued on page 265)

74   The gist of al-Ghazali's discussion is that Allah's customary practice (*sunan Allah*) is to create certain apparent effects in the presence of certain apparent causes. For example, a person who is hungry does not expect that he will be satiated without reaching out and grabbing the food and then eating it. Likewise, people do not expect to have children by merely praying for them. Allah creates the sensation of satiation when food is eaten; Allah brings about children when sexual intercourse occurs; Allah creates burning when fire is brought to cotton. These apparent cause-and-effect relations are created according to the customary practice of Allah. Although Allah is not bound to these customary links between apparent cause and effect, and thus a person could eat and eat and not feel hungry, Jesus could be born to the Virgin Mary, and Abraham could be thrown in the fire and not burn, these are miracles, that is, breaks in the normal links in apparent cause and effect. Miracles are possible and occur when Allah wills, but reliance on miracles is not permitted in Islam. Rather, people are commanded to take the customary means (*khudh al asbab*), but to rely on Allah, not the means. Thus you reach out, grab the food, and eat, but you do not rely on your hand or the food; rather, you rely on Allah, who creates your hand, its motions, the food, and the experience of satiation.

The third pillar of reliance is with regard to actions.

Some ignorant people have supposed that one of the conditions of reliance is to leave working for a living, to stop taking medicine, or to surrender to danger, and this is an error, because it is forbidden according to the sacred law; indeed, the sacred law commends reliance, so how can reliance be obtained via the prohibited?...**74**

When Is Abandoning the Gathering and Storing [of Provisions] Praiseworthy?

Know that abandoning the gathering and storing [of provisions] is praiseworthy for whoever's certainty has become preponderant. As for the one who is weak, whose heart is unsettled, if he does not gather and store [provisions], he will not be able to devote himself exclusively to worship. For such a person, it is best that he turns down the path of the reliant, and not burden himself with that which he is not capable, when the corruption in that with regard to him is greater than the good. Rather, everyone is cured commensurate with his state and power....

75   The two hadith scholars al-Bukhari and Muslim ibn Hajjaj agree upon this hadith's authenticity.

76   Although al-Ghazali was one of the greatest theologians, he did not hesitate to differ with some of the theologians' popularly held theological derivations. Some theologians claimed that love could only be felt for something of one's own species, and hence, since Allah is transcendently beyond similarity to His creation, love is rationally impossible. Al-Ghazali recommends his reader to the more detailed refutation of this found in *The Revival of the Religious Sciences*.

THE EIGHTH FOUNDATION

☐ Love

Allah Most High says in the Qur'an, "O ye who believe! If any from among you turn back from his Faith, soon will Allah produce a people whom He will love as they will love Him" [5:54].

He Most High also says, "Say: If it be that your fathers, your sons, your brothers, your mates, or your kindred; the wealth that ye have gained; the commerce in which ye fear a decline; or the dwellings in which ye delight—are dearer to you than Allah, or His Messenger, or the striving in His cause, then wait until Allah brings about His decision; and Allah guides not the rebellious" [9:24].

The Prophet said, "None of you believes until Allah and His Messenger are more beloved to him than all else."[75]

The Speculative Theologians Deny Love (of Allah) and Metaphorically Interpret It

Most of the theologians deny that a person can love Allah Most High, and instead they metaphorically interpret the term "love," saying it means complying with Allah's commands....[76] However, this was due to their ignorance of the subtleties of these matters....

77   The term used for love throughout is *hubb*, as opposed to the term *'ishq* (passionate love). The latter term is often used by Sufis in their poetry to describe their burning love for Allah, like a burning moth that got too close to its beloved flame. Some scholars objected to the use of the term *'ishq*, because of its association with sensual love and its use in love songs. However, words have linguistic, technical, and cultural meanings, and despite the cultural meanings, the technical meaning of *'ishq* with the Sufis is one they deem appropriate with regard to the love one feels for Allah.

78   Indeed, al-Ghazali reminds us, the delight of the eye is found in a beautiful form, the delight of the ear is found in a beautiful sound, good food pleases the taste buds, a pleasant scent pleases the sense of smell, and the body takes pleasure in soft and clean cloth. All of that is beloved to the soul of the person who is inclined toward them. As for those who do not incline toward such things, al-Ghazali will discuss such people later.

79   Not merely the physical organ, but also the spiritual heart, which perceives and knows, just as we say in English, "I know in my heart."

80   It is the core meaning—that of an inner subtlety that perceives certain nonphysical things—that is the matter at hand, not whether or why some might call it "intellect" or what "sixth senses" implies.

81   In other words, fine scented oils (cologne or perfume) and the lawful and pure companionship of women were two beloved pleasures to the Prophet, perceived through the senses, whereas the ritual prayer's pleasure is spiritually perceived.

What Is the Meaning of a Thing Being Beloved?

Know that every delightful thing is beloved, and the meaning of it being beloved is the inclination of the self toward it. If the inclination is strong, it is called passionate love.[77] The meaning of something being hated is the self's aversion to it due to its being distressing. If the hatred is strong, then the aversion is called loathing.

Know that things that are perceptible to your senses and all of your feelings are either that they are agreeable to you—and it is the delightful thing—or they are negative and disagreeable—and it is the distressing thing. Or they are neither agreeable nor disagreeable; thus such a thing is neither distressing nor delightful. Every delightful thing is beloved to the person who takes pleasure in it, inevitably causing him to have affection for it.

Know that delight follows perception, and there are two types of perception, outward and inward. As for outward perception, it is by way of the five senses.[78] As for inward perception, which is an inner subtlety whose locus is the heart,[79] sometimes this inner subtlety is called the intellect, sometimes spiritual light, and sometimes it is referred to as a sixth sense. But do not look to or contemplate these expressions, as you will fall into error.[80] Rather, the Prophet said, "Of your world, three things have been made beloved to me: scented oils and women, while the ritual prayer has been made the coolness of my eye."[81] Indeed, you know that there is an aspect of scented oils and women that pertains to the sense of smell, touch, and sight, whereas the ritual prayer does not have a portion that pertains to the five senses.

(continued on page 271)

82 Al-Ghazali's explanation of "beautiful inner forms" essentially entails that you have a deep love and appreciation for certain bygone individuals such as the founding legal scholars, certain prominent companions of the Prophet, and the Prophet himself, without ever having seen their external forms. If you examine why you have this love for these bygone individuals, al-Ghazali argues that the answer revolves around three attributes that they possess, namely, their knowledge (of Allah, the angels, the divine revelation, the prophets, the wonders in the spiritual realm, and the subtleties of the prophetic laws), their power (over their egos and desires, and their ability to engage in many acts of worship), and their being purified from major spiritual and character flaws. Indeed, because the Prophet exceeds all others in these attributes, your love for him is even stronger by necessity. If you then turn your attention to the One who created and sent the Prophet, then you will realize that Allah is the source of all good, be it knowledge, spiritual states, or abilities. In other words, through a process of reflection on the ultimate source of all things, your love and appreciation of Allah will increase dramatically, as all things are signs, metaphorically pointing to Allah, and indeed love of Allah is the highest state.

83 Al-Ghazali calls the reader to a high aspiration, that of knowing Allah experientially and loving Him for His majesty, beauty, and the praiseworthiness of His attributes (e.g., omniscience, omnipotence) for which it is inconceivable that they should be possessed by any in addition to Allah. Such a station is that of the perfected and complete person. However, if you fall short of this lofty goal, then you should at bare minimum strive to love Allah for having been generous and good to you, having given you life and all its blessings. The person who fails to even reach this level is lower than a dog, who at least loves his master because of the kindness he bestows.

Rather, it is the portion of the sixth sense whose locus is the heart; no one perceives it who does not have a heart, and Allah intervenes between a person and his heart. Whoever confines himself to the five senses, such a person is like a beast, as the beast also has five senses. The distinguishing characteristic of the human being is the ability to discern with inner insight. The delight of external physical sight is found in beautiful external forms, whereas the delight of inner spiritual insight is found in beautiful inner forms.[82]

Do Not Fall Short of Inclining Toward Allah, the Bestower of Favors

If your spiritual insight falls short of perceiving Allah the Majestic and Perfect, and inclining toward viewing Him and being delighted with Him, and having a strong love for Him, then do not fall short of inclining toward the Bestower of Favors who has been good to you. Do not be lower than the dog, for indeed he loves his owner who is good to him.[83]

84   This is because if the lover loves his beloved's family, city, clothes, and all that he makes and does, his love for all that relates to his beloved is due to its being ascribed to his beloved.

85   Indeed, al-Ghazali mentions that the Prophet Muhammad was the best of creation with regard to goodness toward people, and thus people should naturally incline toward him. The blessing of the Prophet's being sent is traced to Allah, for indeed the Qur'an reminds us that the Prophet did not guide whomever he loved or wished would convert, "rather Allah guides whomever He wills" [28:56]. Therefore, through your inclination toward the Prophet, you realize that he is ultimately a gift from Allah, and thus your love of Allah must necessarily increase.

86   Whatever the gnostic loves is because it can ultimately be traced through a chain of love to Allah. Everything is from Allah, so ultimate love is for Allah alone. The Qur'an teaches that all things in creation hymn or recite the praises of Allah and that they are instructive signs for those who reflect. The companions love the Prophet because of his love for Allah. Allah loves the Prophet, and the Prophet loves his companions. The person who loves for the sake of Allah enters into a cycle of love, of loving and being beloved.

The Gnostic Does Not Love Anyone Except Allah Most High

The gnostic does not love anyone except Allah. If he loves other than Allah, it is that he loves him *for* Allah Mighty and Majestic.[84]

Everything that exists is the creation and ordering of Allah Mighty and Majestic, and all things are the slaves of Allah Most High. If you love the messenger, you love him because he is the beloved messenger of his Beloved.[85] If you love the companions of the Prophet, it is because they are beloved to Allah's messenger and they assiduously obeyed him.

If you love food, it is because it strengthens your mount by which you reach your beloved, by which I mean the body. If you love looking at flowers, rivers, lights, and beautiful forms, it is because they are the handiwork of your Beloved, and because they are signs pointing to His beauty and majesty.[86]

87 The delight that you feel from a given experience is in accordance with the desire you felt for this experience. Because the gnostic desires the experience of the Divine Presence, the delight will be as great as the strength of his desire. The desire will be very high, because the object of desire—the experience of the Divine—is so lofty.

88 Marmaduke Pickthall's translation has been used here, instead of Yusuf Ali's, as it better preserves the use of the word *Ruh* ("spirit" or "soul"), which Yusuf Ali leaves out.

89 Al-Ghazali explains that a child first desires things like food, but as he reaches maturity he begins to desire marriage and intercourse, and his strong desire for food is eclipsed. Later, such a person may become less interested in marriage, and his desire then focuses on achieving a high rank in society, fame, and power. But if he is fortunate, he may move beyond this to desire spiritual knowledge of Allah, causing all his previous desires to be eclipsed. Of course, each individual is different, and not all people will move up this ladder of desires, and of course some may begin to climb it but stall at the love of power and fame. Al-Ghazali likens the person who does not desire spiritual knowledge to a person struck with an illness that causes him to lose the desire for food, eventually causing death. Indeed the spiritual heart can die if it does not receive the nourishment of spiritual knowledge.

The Delight of the Gnostic in the World

Know that the delight of the gnostic in the world is from the witnessing of the Divine Presence's beauty, more so than from all the other delights he conceives in the world other than it. That is because the delight is commensurate with the desire, and the strength of the desire is commensurate with the agreeability of the object of desire.[87]

Likewise, the most suitable things for the bodies are nourishing foods, and the most appropriate of things for the hearts is spiritual knowledge of Allah [gnosis], and indeed, gnosis is the nourishment of the heart, and by "heart" I mean the Divine Soul, about which Allah Most High says, "Say: 'The soul is from the affair of my Lord'" [17:85] and "When I have fashioned him (in due proportion) and breathed into him of My spirit" [15:29], and he attributes this soul to Himself. This soul is not for beasts, or those humans whose state is like that of beasts; rather, Allah elects for it the prophets and the saints, and with that He Most High says, "And thus have We inspired in thee (Muhammad) a Spirit[88] of Our command. Thou knewest not what the Scripture was, nor what the Faith. But We have made it a light whereby We guide whom We will of Our bondmen. And lo! thou verily dost guide unto a right path" [42:52].

Spiritual knowledge of Allah is the most appropriate of things for this soul, because the most appropriate for each thing is its unique trait. Indeed, beautiful sound is not appropriate for sight, because it is not from its unique traits. The unique trait of the human soul is knowledge of the spiritual realities. The more noble the thing known, the more delightful the knowledge of it. There is nothing more noble than Allah, nor anything more majestic than He, so knowledge of Him, and knowledge of His attributes, His entity, and the wonders of the physical and spiritual worlds are the most delightful of things to the heart. This is because the desire for this is the strongest of desires, and with that it was created last, after the rest of the desires, and every desire that comes after another is stronger than what comes before it....[89]

90 Al-Ghazali's firm conviction is that the inhabitants of heaven will "see Allah" in a way that does not imply limitations or containment. Since the human eye is currently only capable of witnessing bodies contained by the six directions, "seeing Allah" sounds inappropriate to some. However, Allah is the creator of the human eye. Allah can create it to function differently in the afterlife, so it will have the capacity to witness Allah, but not in a way that attributes direction or limitations to Allah. Since we have not experienced this, it is "currently not possible" to understand how it will occur. In any case, the eyes' witnessing of Allah in the afterlife will be far more delightful than the soul's witnessing of Allah in this life.

The Delight of Gazing at the Countenance of Allah the Most Generous

This spiritual knowledge of Allah [gnosis], even if its delight is substantial, it has no relation to the delight of gazing at the countenance of Allah the Most Generous in the afterlife; that cannot be conceived in this world because it is a secret whose disclosure is currently not possible.[90]

It is not appropriate that you understand from the term "gaze" that which the masses and theologians understand from it, for its implication necessitates direction and spatial relation....

However, it is necessary that you understand that the conception of the Divine Presence and its wondrous array of splendor, exaltedness, majesty, and grandeur is imprinted on the heart of the gnostic, just as the conception of the sensory world, for example, is impressed in your senses, as though you look at it even if your eyes are closed....

The Delight of Gazing at Allah Is Greater Than the Delight of Gnosis

If you were to look at the object of your intense love from behind a thin curtain at the time of unveiling and in a state of weak light, and at a state in which beneath your clothes were scorpions and hornets, stinging and preoccupying you, it is obvious that your delight in witnessing your beloved would be weak. If all at one moment the sun shone, the thin curtain were lifted, and the scorpions and hornets were to depart from you, and profound, excessive, and intense love were to rush upon you, there is no relation between this magnanimous delight that overtakes you now with that love that was with you before. With that, you understand that there is no relation between the delight of gazing at Allah in the afterlife with the delight of gnosis (in this world), for indeed it is much greater than that....

91   Ultimately, you must purify your heart of desires for other than gnosis, through purifying your heart of base traits and attachments. A pure heart is necessary in order to experience the ultimate realities of Sufism.

Why Does Desire for Spiritual Knowledge of Allah Most High Weaken?

Desire for spiritual knowledge of Allah Most High weakens because it is crowded by the rest of the desires....[91]

There Are Many Signs of Love

Know that there are many signs of love, including putting the affairs of Allah before the desires of the self, being cautiously pious, and keeping to the limits of the sacred law. Also among the signs of love is longing for meeting Allah, being free from dislike of death, except for the person who desires to increase in gnosis, for indeed the delight of witnessing Allah is commensurate with the perfection and completion of gnosis. Indeed, gnosis is the seed of witnessing. Additionally, from among the signs of love is contentment with divine destiny. So we shall now mention the meaning of contentment so that person will not be deceived by that which he finds in his self from the notions that occur to his mind, such that he thinks that it is the reality of love for Allah Most High, for indeed that is very scarce.

92   Both the terms "select" and "choose" have the implication of being "one of the select" or "one of the chosen" in the sense of being among the elect, chosen by Allah.

93   This is analogous to an angry person who gets in a fight and does not feel the pain of the strikes of his opponent until later when he has calmed down. How then could a person who has witnessed the beauty of the Divine Presence not be too astonished to perceive the temporary hardships of this life?

94   Such a person is similar to one who is ill but is content that taking medicine is a means to curing it.

THE NINTH FOUNDATION

☐ Contentment with Divine Destiny

Allah Most High says in the Qur'an, "Allah will say, 'This is a day on which the truthful will profit from their truth; theirs are gardens, with rivers flowing beneath—their eternal Home. Allah is well pleased with them, and they with Allah. That is the great salvation, (the fulfillment of all desires)" [5:119].

The Prophet said, "If Allah loves someone, He tests him with tribulations, and if he is patient, Allah selects him, and if he is content, Allah chooses him."[92]

How Is Contentment Conceived?

A group of people denied contentment and said, "Contentment is not conceivable in that which contravenes desire; rather, only patience is conceivable." Moreover, they were drawn into this ruinous conclusion by denying love. Whereas we affirm love, and its sign is contentment with tribulation, and with that which contravenes a person's nature and desire; this is conceivable from three perspectives:

1. The first is that witnessing love astonishes him such that he does not perceive feelings of suffering....[93]

2. The second is that he feels suffering and is naturally disinclined toward it but is content in his intellect and faith due to his knowledge of the abundance of reward associated with under-going tribulations....[94]

(continued on page 283)

95 Al-Ghazali gives the example of the Prophet Moses who traveled with al-Khidr and witnessed shocking and troubling things, which, upon having their wisdom explained, were no longer shocking. (For details, see *Surah* 18:60–82.)

96 As mentioned previously, the theory of acquisition (*kasb*) is that all actions and their effects are created by Allah, and you are held accountable for choosing the action and its expected effects. Your "acquisition" is that you acquire the reward or punishment for choosing a particular action, even though Allah is the one who ultimately brings about the effects. So if you choose to throw a ball through your neighbor's window, you are held accountable for choosing that action, despite the fact that on the level of ultimate reality, Allah created the ball, your arm, its movement, the window, the effect of breaking glass, and so on.

3. The third perspective on contentment is that he believes that under every shocking thing there are subtle realities from Allah, and that causes all opposition in the form of asking "why?" or "how?" to exit from his heart....[95]

How Do You Join between Contentment with the Divine Decree and Detesting Disbelief?

Perhaps you might say, "How do I join between contentment with the Divine Decree and detesting disbelief and disobedience, which the sacred law has obligated us to do?"

Know that contentment and discontentment are in conflict if they befall a thing from one direction. If you were to kill your enemy who is also the enemy of another of your enemies, then you would be content with that from the perspective that he was your enemy, and discontent from the angle that he was the enemy of your other enemy.

With that, with regard to disobedience there are two perspectives:

1. The first is with regard to Allah Most High, such that the act of disobedience is from His Divine Decree, and from this perspective it is something with which to be content.

2. The second is with regard to the disobedient one, such that the act of disobedience is ascribed to him and is his acquisition,[96] and it is a sign of his being detested by Allah. From this angle, it is something with which to be discontented.

97   Instead, al-Ghazali instructs that one prays to Allah in order to worship Him, draw nearer to Him, purify and soften the heart, achieve presence of heart, and prepare it for spiritual subtleties and lights.

98   That is to say that Allah has made eating a means to satiation, studying a means to acquiring knowledge, striking a match a means to producing a spark, despite the fact that He is the Creator of the apparent cause and the apparent effect. Likewise, Allah has made supplicatory prayer a means to nearness, presence of heart, and preparing the heart for the reception of divine graces and spiritual lights.

Joining between Contentment with the Divine Decree and Taking the Means

With that, it is necessary that you do not suppose that the meaning of contentment with the Divine Decree is leaving supplicatory prayer, or leaving seeking medicinal cures, or ignoring the arrow that is shot at you such that it hits you when you have the power to deflect it with a shield.[97]

From among the things that constitute contentment with the Divine Decree is that whatever Allah has made a means to what is beloved to Him is approached by their physical causes.[98] Indeed, leaving such means is in contradiction to what is beloved to Him and in sharp contrast to His approval. It is not from contentment that a person who is thirsty does not extend his hand toward cold water, erroneously alleging that he is content with the thirst that Allah Most High has decreed for him. Rather, it is from the decree of Allah Most High, and His love, that thirst is lifted with water.

Contentment with the Divine Decree is by no means that which entails leaving from the confines of the sacred law and the auspices of the way of Allah Most High; rather, its meaning is leaving opposition to Allah Most High, outwardly and inwardly, with the expending of effort from His servant in attaining Allah's love. That is accomplished by keeping to what is commanded and leaving what is prohibited.

99 Those stations that are sought in order to bring one nearer to Allah, as mentioned below, can be achieved through the remembrance of death. Remembering that life will one day come to an end, after which each soul will be judged, reminds us that our beliefs and actions matter and will have an impact on our ultimate state. A person who remembers death is more likely to turn in repentance to Allah, to abstain from matters that distance him or her from Allah out of fear of Allah's punishment, and to patiently persevere in acts of worship, hardship, and refusing to heed the call to his or her base desires.

THE TENTH FOUNDATION

☐ Remembering Death and Its Reality, and the Categories of Spiritual Punishments

Know that the nine stations that we mentioned above are not on one rank or level.**99** Rather, some of them are sought in and of themselves—such as love and contentment, indeed they are the highest stations—and some of them are sought for the sake of other than themselves, such as repentance, abstinence, fear, and patience. This is because:

- Repentance is to return from the way of being distant, in order to approach the way of nearness.

- Abstinence is leaving that which preoccupies you away from nearness.

- Fear is a whip that drives you to leave those things that preoccupy you.

- Patience is the struggle with desires that block the path to nearness.

All of the aforementioned are not sought in and of themselves, but rather what is sought is nearness to Allah, which in turn is achieved via gnosis and love. Gnosis and love are sought in and of themselves, not for something other than themselves. However, that is not accomplished except by cutting from the heart the love of other than Allah Most High, and fear, patience, and abstinence are needed for that.

(continued on page 289)

287

100 The word for "remember" (*dhakara*) can also mean "mention" or "remembrance." Both are intended: however, al-Ghazali in the following phrase says, "With that, we have mentioned [*awradna*] it, and the sacred law extols the merits for its mention [*dhikr*]." Indeed, the purpose of its mention here is to aid you in remembering death and, in doing so, to spoil your love of the world and cut the attachments of the heart to it. This final chapter in al-Ghazali's text is rather lengthy, yet very important. However, with great difficulty it has been shortened, with some of its main points being summarized in the annotations.

101 This hadith's authenticity is agreed upon by the two hadith scholars al-Bukhari and Muslim ibn Hajjaj.

102 Al-Ghazali elucidates this point, saying that the gnostics perceive the states and blessings of the afterlife, and the beauty of the Divine Presence, but it as though they witness it from behind a fine curtain in dim light. They long to see it in reality, and they know that this is not possible except in death. Therefore, they do not dislike death, because they do not dislike meeting Allah Most High.

From the great matters that are useful with regard to achieving the aforementioned stations is the remembrance[100] of death. With that, we have mentioned it, and the sacred law extols the merits for its mention, for by it your love of the world is spoiled, the attachments of the heart to the world are cut.

Allah Most High says in the Qur'an, "Say: 'The Death from which ye flee will truly overtake you; then will ye be sent back to the Knower of things secret and open, and He will tell you (the truth of) the things that ye did!'" [62:8].

The Prophet said, "Whoever detests meeting Allah, Allah detests meeting him."[101]

Death Is Dreadfully Tremendous, and That Which Follows It Is Even More So

Know that death is dreadfully tremendous, yet what follows it is more tremendous than it. In its mention there is much benefit, for it spoils and makes loathsome the world, making it hateful to the heart. Hating the world is the apex of every good, just as loving it is the apex of every sin.

There are two benefits to the gnostic in mentioning death:

1. The first is aversion to the world.
2. The second is longing for the afterlife.[102]

There is no cause for people's approaching and having concern for this world except a scarcity of contemplation on death. The way of contemplating death is that you empty your heart of all thoughts except those pertaining to death, while sitting in isolation and taking up the remembrance of death in the innermost core of your heart....

103 Prolonged hope and procrastination entail thinking you will have time to do sometime in the future, when the future is not guaranteed to anyone.

104 Annihilation in the Oneness of Allah, as mentioned in different ways previously, is to lose your awareness of anything other than Allah, even to the extent that you are not even aware of yourself or your surroundings. Such terms are sometimes used differently by different Sufis, to the extent that one word might have multiple definitions and usages, or one meaning might be signified by multiple words. Where there is overlap, that is, one word being used for different meanings, or different words being used for one meaning, misunderstandings often follow. For this reason, one Sufi might chastise another for use of a term that each understands differently, and centuries of disagreement ensue. That said, I understand al-Ghazali's use of annihilation in the Oneness of Allah to be synonymous with his general usage of the term "annihilation."

105 That is, a person who is not shackled by past regrets or future worldly hopes. "His moment" is defined by whatever state comes to him by Allah's divine plan, and he is in it, assiduously observing the commands of the sacred law.

The Root of Heedlessness Is Prolonged Hope

The root of heedlessness is having prolonged hope,[103] and this is the essence of ignorance.... The Prophet said, "Indeed the most dreadful of things that I fear for my nation are two characteristics: following vain desires and having prolonged hope...."

The Perfected Gnostic Is in No Need of Remembering Death

Know that the perfected gnostic who is infatuated with the remembrance of Allah Most High is in no need of remembering death; rather, his state is total annihilation in the Oneness of Allah.[104] He does not turn to the past or the present, ... rather he is the "son of his moment...."[105]

Consequently, the remembrance of death is needed by the person whose heart is inclined toward this world, in order that he knows that he will part with it....

106 Here al-Ghazali seems to be distinguishing between the soul that continues after death and is the locus of gnosis and what we might call the life force that animates living things and carries capacities of the senses. This life force is what, according to al-Ghazali and the medieval conceptions of medicine at the time, "emanates from the heart, and spreads out through the rest of the body, in the hollow cavities of the arteries." It is, perhaps, similar to Taoist conceptions of chi. The science that deals with this life-force soul is the science of medicine, whereas the science that deals with the soul that is the locus of gnosis and does not terminate at death is the science of Sufism.

107 By "faithfulness" al-Ghazali intends the soul that assumes the obligation of *taklif*. *Taklif* is being charged with the duties of Islamic law, such as belief, prayer, fasting, and so on. The conditions of *taklif* include being sane, having reached puberty (or the age of fifteen, whichever comes first), and having heard a proper and comprehensive description of the truths of Islam. If you are charged with the duties of Islam (*mukallaf*), you can be rewarded for your good actions or punished for your bad actions. A person who is not sane, has not reached puberty (or the age of fifteen), or has not received the proper message of Islam is not held accountable for his or her actions or beliefs in the afterlife, but is rather, according to some scholars, granted paradise, while other scholars believe that such a person will be given the test in the afterlife that determines his or her final abode.

108 The sacred law does not permit mentioning the detailed explanation of the attributes of this soul, so very little has been mentioned about it. Instead, al-Ghazali will mention something of the soul experiences after death, according to what is permitted by the sacred law.

109 Al-Ghazali continues with a rather lengthy exposition of various states after death, including those in the grave and in the afterlife. Ghazali's views on death and the afterlife have been summarized in the Introduction. See page xxiv.

The Reality of Death and Its Nature

Perhaps you desire to know the reality of death and its nature. You will never know that unless you know the reality of life, and you will never know the reality of life unless you know the reality of the soul, which is your very self and your reality. Indeed, the soul is the most concealed of things from you, and you cannot expect to know your Lord before you know your self. By "self" I mean your soul that is the special affair that is attributed to Allah Most High when He says in the Qur'an, "Say: 'The soul is from the affair of my Lord'" [17:85] and "When I have fashioned him (in due proportion) and breathed into him of My spirit" [15:29]. This is not to be confused with *the subtle corporeal soul,*[106] ... for indeed beasts also have this type of soul, which is effaced at death. This corporeal soul is not the locus of gnosis and faithfulness; rather, that which is the carrier of faithfulness is the specific soul of the human being....[107] This soul does not die nor is it annihilated; rather, it remains after death, either in a state of comfort and felicity or in a state of hell and misery. This soul is the locus of gnosis. The earth by no means devours the locus of faithfulness and gnosis, as is mentioned in various reports and witnessed by the witnessing of those of spiritual insight.[108]

The Soul Is Not Annihilated at Death

This soul is never annihilated, nor does it die; rather, with death it only exchanges its state and home, advancing from one home to another. The grave is, with regard to the soul and its home, either a garden from the gardens of paradise or a pit from the pits of hellfire....[109]

So be satisfied with what has been mentioned here, for indeed it almost exceeds the limits of a book such as this, and so we abridge it thus and with it we close the discussion of the Forty Foundations. Whoever seeks more information on this topic, let them seek it from the chapter on remembering death as found in *The Revival of the Religious Sciences*.

110 That is, you did not listen from the depths of your heart.

111 Inspect your motivations and excuses, and counter them with the wisdom in these chapters. It is common for Sufis past and present to take note of their sins and to revisit them at the end of the day to determine their motivations and seek repentance for them. For more information, al-Ghazali refers his reader to the chapter on taking account of and watching over one's actions (*muhasibah* and *muraqabah*) in *The Revival of the Religious Sciences*.

112 Al-Ghazali ends his text with a customary prayer, seeking Allah's help and forgiveness, as well as seeking Allah's blessings upon the Prophet.

□ Conclusion

Know that we have warned you and awakened your desire. So if you are adverse to being attentive or you were paying attention merely with the outward aspect of your heart,[110] as you listen to formal speech, then indeed you have failed and lost, and you do not oppress any except your own self.

Allah Most High says in the Qur'an, "And who doth more wrong than one who is reminded of the Signs of his Lord, but turns away from them, forgetting the [deeds] that his hands have sent forth? Verily We have set veils over their hearts lest they should understand this, and over their ears, deafness, if thou callest them to guidance, even then will they never accept guidance" [18:57].

If you were attentive with the attentiveness of the one who possesses intelligence and sharp sight, and if you reflected with the reflection of one who has a prepared heart,... then leave the entirety of that which diverts you from the straight path, and nothing diverts you from it except love of the *dunya* and heedlessness of Allah Most High and the Last Day. Strive to fully devote your heart every day for an hour after the morning prayer, with a pure mind. So contemplate your state of affairs, and consider your point of origin and your destination, and take your self to account....[111]

If you desire to know the path of inspecting your self, watching over it, taking it to account, and rebuking it, then seek that from the Book of Taking to Account and Rebuking in *The Revival of the Religious Sciences*, for this book cannot bear the likes of it.

May Allah Most High grant us all success, and guide us by His Grace, Generosity, and Munificence to the path of Truth and His support. May the peace and blessing of Allah be upon our liege-lord Muhammad, and upon his family and companions.[112]

Epilogue □

Here too ends the abridged translation and commentary on al-Ghazali's *The Forty Foundations of Religion*. Although divided into four sections, the latter two are subsections of a single dimension, that is, the dimension of Islam that pertains to the soul. The religion of Islam is divided into three dimensions, that of the beliefs held in the mind (called *Iman*), the laws of the body as it pertains to ritual and society (called *Islam*), and the dimension of the perfection and purification of the soul (called *Ihsan*). The first section of this book summarized the core beliefs of the Muslim. The second section summarized the core practices and actions of the Muslim. The third and fourth sections respectively dealt with the purification of the base traits of the soul and the adornment of the soul with meritorious states and traits. The first dimension is the realm of theology, the second is the realm of law, and the third is the realm of Sufism, or Islamic spirituality. That al-Ghazali devoted the majority of his book to this dimension and that he saw this book as possessing the marrow or essence of the Qur'anic teachings indicate that he viewed the perfection and purification of the soul as paramount to the religion of Islam, as it contains within it the incitement to perfect a person's faith and practice. Al-Ghazali's scholarship in law, theology, Sufism, and philosophy has had a profound effect on the history of Islam and the Judeo-Christian tradition as well. It is hoped that the previous pages offer the reader a brief glimpse into but a few examples of al-Ghazali's many contributions to the intellectual and spiritual history of humankind. All errors are my own; all perfections are from Allah. All praise is due to Allah Most High, may peace and blessings be sent upon His beloved Prophet.

Notes ☐

Foreword: Al-Ghazali and the Tradition of Islamic Renewal

1. Every prophet is distinguished with certain attributes such as truthfulness, trustworthiness, sinlessness, wisdom and discretion in the highest degree, conveyance of God's messages, and freedom from any mental or physical impediment.

2. In the case of almost complete deviations and for an overall revival, God sent one from among the five greatest of messengers (Noah, Abraham, Moses, Jesus, and Muhammad, upon them be God's peace), to whom He gave a book which contained the principles of belief, worship, good conduct, and the rules of human social life. When people began to stray from the way of God or strayed to a lesser extent, He sent prophets to guide people back to it in the footsteps of the previous messenger. However, if the deviation covered a considerable distance or people needed more powerful guidance for straightforward travel on the way of God, God sent messengers such as Hud, Salih, Shu'ayb, and Lot in the former case, and David, Solomon, Jonah, Job, and Eliach, upon them all be God's peace, in the latter, and gave them scriptures which usually contained advice, encouragement and discouragement, prayers, supplication, and litanies.

3. According to many researchers, such great caliphs or statesmen as Umar ibn 'Abd al-'Aziz (679–720) from the Umayyads, Abu 'Abdu'llah Muhammad Mahdi ibn al-Mansur (742–785) from the Abbasids, and Sultan Mehmet II (1432–1481) and Sultan Salim I (1470–1520) from the Ottoman sultans can be and have generally been accepted as revivers in the field of government, while great scholars such as Abu Abu'l-Hasan al-Ash'ari (873–935), Abu Ishak al-Isfarani (d. 1027), Abu Bakr Muhammad ibn Ahmad al-Sarakhsi (1009–1090), 'Abd al-Qadir al-Jilani (1077–1166), Imam Fakhr al-Din al-Razi (1149–1210), Abu'l-Hasan 'Ali al-Shazili (1196–1257), Taj al-Din 'Abd al-Wahhab ibn 'Ali al-Subki (1327–1370), Sa'd al-Din al-Taftazani (1322–1390), 'Abd al-Wahhab ibn Ahmad al-Sha'rani (1492–1565), Jalal al-Din al-Suyuti (1445–1505), and many others have come at critical points in Islamic history and rendered great services by God's leave to restore Islamic life and guide people to true belief, worship, and action.

4. Two other famous and most widely accepted ones among revivers or renewers are Imam al-Rabbani Ahmad Faruq al-Sirhindi (1564–1624) and Bediuzzaman Said Nursi (1877–1960).

   Imam al-Rabbani, who lived in India and is mostly known for his *Maktubat* (The Letters), is called *Mujaddid Alf Sani* (The Renewer of the Second Millennium). His movement of renewal or revival was usually in the field of cleansing Islamic faith and Sufism of the un-Islamic elements that found their way into Islam mainly through certain deviant sects. However, his movement was not restricted only to this field, but rather also affected Islamic law. (The emperor Shah Alamgir [1618–1707] was brought up and educated by Muhammad Ma'sum al-Faruqi, the son of Imam al-Rabbani. Shah Alamgir formed a committee of scholars and had them prepare the most voluminous collection of Islamic religious rulings concerning all fields of life, which is known as *Fatawa-yi Alamgiriya* or *Fatawa-yi Hindiya*.

Bediuzzaman Said Nursi came in the most critical period of not only Muslim history but also the history of the world. He witnessed the collapse of the Islamic caliphate and the Ottoman state, and the dissolution or disintegration of the Muslim world after the colonization of many Muslim lands from the Philippines to Morocco, and the foundation of the Turkish Republic. Materialism was triumphant, communism was popular, and Muslims were being urged to reject Islam. Shocked by the West's scientific and military victories and influenced by modern thought, Muslims were discarding their roots and sometimes their belief. Many intellectuals pursued un-Islamic ideas. Science and philosophy were used to produce young atheists, and nihilism was popular. Such things were done in the name of civilization, modernization, and contemporary thinking. At just this juncture, Said Nursi started a movement of revival in thinking, belief, worship, action, and individual religious life. In the history of Islam, the revival or renewal movements of Bediuzzaman Said Nursi and Imam al-Ghazali are very similar to each other.

5. Their definitions of Sufism could be summarized as follows: Sufism is the path followed by an individual who, having been able to free himself or herself from human vices and weaknesses in order to acquire angelic qualities and conduct pleasing to God, lives in accordance with the requirements of God's knowledge and love, and in the spiritual delight that ensues.

The works such as *A Book on Observing God's Rights* by Harith al-Muhasibi (781–857), who would have considerable influence on al-Ghazali; *A Description of the Way of the People of Sufism* by Abu Bakr Muhammad ibn Ishaq al-Kalabazi (d. 990?); *Book of Lights* by Abu Nasr 'Abdu'llah ibn 'Ali al-Tusi al-Sarraj (d. 959/60 or 988); *The Nourishment of Hearts in Relationship with the Beloved and the Description of the Seeker's Way to the Station of Unity* by Abu Talib al-Makki (d. 997); and *The Epistle to the Sufis* by 'Abd al-Karim ibn Hawazin al-Qushayri (986–1074), who was a famous scholar of *hadith* and interpreter of the Qur'an, were among the precious sources that discussed Islamic Sufism according to the Qur'an and the *sunnah* and as a way that every Muslim can and should follow in everyday life.

6. Nizamiyyah schools were schools of higher education founded by and named after Abu 'Ali al-Hasan al-Tusi (1018–1092), known as Nizam al-Mulk (The Order of the State), the famous Seljuk vizier who served the two greatest of Seljuk sultans, Alp Arslan (1063–1072) and Malik Shah (1072–1092),

organized the Seljuk governmental bodies, and bridged the gap between the 'Abbasids and the Seljuks against the Fatimids and the Buyids.

7. We should, however, note here that, as respectable Dr. Aaron Spevack, the translator of al-Ghazali's *The Forty Foundations of Religion*, rightly points out, "al-Ghazali was not critical of the entirety of the philosophical tradition" or rational or reflective thought. It is not possible that any Muslim scholar, particularly one like al-Ghazali, can be against rational or reflective thought, while the Qur'an orders human beings to think, reflect, ponder, contemplate, reason, behold, understand, perceive, make comparisons, deduce, take heed, and consider in many of its verses.

8. Actually, there was no substantial disagreement, and it should not have been viewed as a disagreement, for it only involved dealing with different aspects and elements of religion under different titles.

Introduction

1. The primary point of departure for the Sunnis and the Shia was a disagreement over who was the rightful heir to rule over the Muslim community after the death of the Prophet Muhammad in 633 CE. The Shia argued that Ali, the cousin of the Prophet, should have ruled, while the Sunnis claimed that the Prophet's companion Abu Bakr rightfully took control of the political reins. Additional differences, theological and legal, emerged over time, and within the Shia sect, a number of subsects came into being, including the Ismaili, who were in direct political conflict with the Sunni Seljuks.

2. Al-Shafi'i was a prominent jurist who died in the ninth century CE. He founded a school of legal deduction (*madhhab*), to which al-Ghazali later belonged. Al-Ghazali achieved a high level of capability with al-Shafi'i's legal methodology and did not merely quote and blindly follow all al-Shafi'i's deductions. Indeed, al-Ghazali often differed with al-Shafi'i's deductions, even though he used the same basic methodology.

Selected Bibliography ☐

Gassick, Trevor, Muneer Goolam Fareed, and Isma'il Ibn Kathir. *The Life of the Prophet Muhammad: Al-Sira al-Nabawiyya*. Reading, UK: Garnet, 2006.

Griffel, Frank. "Al-Ghazali." In *The Stanford Encyclopedia of Philosophy*, Fall 2008 ed., ed. Edward N. Zalta. http://plato.stanford.edu/archives/fall2008/entries/al-ghazali.

———. *Al-Ghazali's Philosophical Theology*. Oxford: Oxford University Press, 2009.

McCarthy, Richard Joseph. *Deliverance from Error: An Annotated Translation of "Al-Munqidh min al Dalal" and Other Relevant Works of Al-Ghazali*. Louisville, KY: Fons Vitae, 1999.

Pickthall, Marmaduke William. *The Meaning of the Holy Quran: An Explanatory Translation*. Bombay, India: Bilal Books, 1997.

Qushayri, Abu al-Qasim. *Principles of Sufism*. Translated by B. R. Schlegell. Berkeley, CA: Mizan Press, 1992.

www.ghazali.org.

About SKYLIGHT PATHS Publishing

SkyLight Paths Publishing is creating a place where people of different spiritual traditions come together for challenge and inspiration, a place where we can help each other understand the mystery that lies at the heart of our existence.

Through spirituality, our religious beliefs are increasingly becoming a part of our lives—rather than *apart* from our lives. While many of us may be more interested than ever in spiritual growth, we may be less firmly planted in traditional religion. Yet, we do want to deepen our relationship to the sacred, to learn from our own as well as from other faith traditions, and to practice in new ways.

SkyLight Paths sees both believers and seekers as a community that increasingly transcends traditional boundaries of religion and denomination—people wanting to learn from each other, *walking together, finding the way.*

For your information and convenience, at the back of this book we have provided a list of other SkyLight Paths books you might find interesting and useful. They cover the following subjects:

Buddhism / Zen	Global Spiritual	Monasticism
Catholicism	Perspectives	Mysticism
Children's Books	Gnosticism	Poetry
Christianity	Hinduism /	Prayer
Comparative	Vedanta	Religious Etiquette
Religion	Inspiration	Retirement
Current Events	Islam / Sufism	Spiritual Biography
Earth-Based	Judaism	Spiritual Direction
Spirituality	Kabbalah	Spirituality
Enneagram	Meditation	Women's Interest
	Midrash Fiction	Worship

Or phone, fax, mail or e-mail to: SKYLIGHT PATHS Publishing
Sunset Farm Offices, Route 4 • P.O. Box 237 • Woodstock, Vermont 05091
Tel: (802) 457-4000 • Fax: (802) 457-4004 • www.skylightpaths.com
Credit card orders: (800) 962-4544 (8:30AM–5:30PM ET Monday–Friday)
Generous discounts on quantity orders. SATISFACTION GUARANTEED. Prices subject to change.